BENCHMARKS

TERRY EASTLAND is the editor of *Forbes MediaCritic* and a fellow at the Ethics and Public Policy Center. He is the author of *Energy in the Executive: The Case for the Strong Presidency* (The Free Press, 1992) and *Ethics, Politics, and the Independent Counsel: Executive Power, Executive Vice 1789-1989.*

BENCHMARKS

Great Constitutional Controversies
in the Supreme Court

Edited by
TERRY EASTLAND

Foreword by
GRIFFIN B. BELL

ETHICS AND PUBLIC POLICY CENTER
WASHINGTON, D.C.

WILLIAM B. EERDMANS PUBLISHING COMPANY
GRAND RAPIDS, MICHIGAN

Copyright © 1995 by the Ethics and Public Policy Center
1015 Fifteenth St. N.W., Washington, D.C., 20005

Published jointly 1995 by the Ethics and Public Policy Center and
Wm. B. Eerdmans Publishing Co.
255 Jefferson Ave. S.E., Grand Rapids, Michigan 49503

00 99 98 97 96 95   7 6 5 4 3 2 1

Printed in the United States of America

Library of Congress Cataloging-in-Publication Data

Benchmarks : great constitutional controversies in the
Supreme Court / edited by Terry Eastland ;
foreword by Griffin B. Bell.
p.   cm.
Includes index.
Includes bibliographical references.
ISBN 0-8028-3771-9 (cloth)
1. United States—Constitutional law—Interpretation and
construction.   2. Judicial review—United States.
I. Eastland, Terry.
KF4550.B375   1995
342.73'02—dc20   94-43332
[347.3022]   CIP

Contents

Foreword

GRIFFIN B. BELL

In the Constitution's familiar allocation of the powers of the federal government, it is Article III that treats the judicial power. Here a reader learns that "the judicial Power shall be vested in one supreme Court" as well as any inferior courts Congress wishes to establish—and of course has established. What the reader does not find, in Article III or anywhere else in the Constitution, is specific mention of the power of judicial or constitutional review—the power by which federal courts examine acts of the federal and state governments for their conformity to the Constitution.

This omission does not mean the power is illegitimate. In the 1780s, state courts exercised judicial review as a means of restraining state legislatures, and most members of the Constitutional Convention in 1787 thought that some form of this power was available to the government established by the new Constitution. More importantly, the power may be inferred from the text and nature of the Constitution. There are two relevant texts. Article III also says that "[t]he judicial Power shall extend to all Cases, in Law and Equity, arising under this Constitution." And Article IV declares (in what is called the Supremacy Clause) that the Constitution "shall be the supreme Law of the Land."

In *Federalist* 78 Alexander Hamilton fleshed out the inferential argument for judicial review. Because the Constitution is "fundamental law," Hamilton wrote, it must be superior to what is done by the legislature. As he put it, "the intention of the people"—the Consti-

---

Griffin B. Bell was attorney general of the United States from 1977 to 1979.

tution—must be superior to "the intention of their agents." Therefore, he concluded, "[n]o legislative act . . . contrary to the Constitution can be valid."

Necessarily, some department of government must have the power to decide whether "the intention of [the people's] agents" violates the "intention of the people." Hamilton said the judiciary was that department. Why the judiciary? Hamilton contended that it does not make sense to suppose that members of the legislature should be "the constitutional judges of their own powers"; it is "far more rational," he said, "to suppose that the courts were designed to be an intermediate body between the people and the legislature in order, among other things, to keep the latter within the limits assigned to their authority." The very character of the judiciary, Hamilton said, makes it suited to this task. Unlike the legislature, it does not make the laws, and unlike the executive, it does not enforce the laws (or command the troops). Rather, it judges. And judging involves interpretation— an intellectual task.

Hamilton's argument for judicial review may be summarized as follows, using his own words: Because "[t]he interpretation of the laws [including the Constitution] is the proper and peculiar province of the courts," the judiciary is charged with "the duty . . . to declare all [legislative] acts contrary to the manifest tenor of the Constitution void."

The first case in which the Supreme Court declared a legislative act contrary to the Constitution and therefore void was decided in 1803. This was *Marbury* v. *Madison,* in which the Court found unconstitutional a section of the Judiciary Act of 1789. *Marbury* is famous, not for its facts, which are seldom remembered any more, but for Chief Justice John Marshall's defense of judicial review. Marshall's argument was similar in some respects to Hamilton's, as it recognized the Constitution as "the fundamental and paramount law," which the courts must enforce. Marshall declared: "It is emphatically the province and duty of the judicial department to say what the law is." And if in a given case a law is in conflict with the Constitution, the Constitution must prevail.

Hamilton and Marshall saw judicial review as a means of ensuring that Congress—which they and their colleagues regarded as the branch of government potentially the most dangerous to liberty—

abided by the terms of the Constitution. Yet in retrospect it is clear that, even on the terms by which judicial review was originally understood, the courts' exercise of this power could not be limited to cases challenging acts of Congress. After all, Congress isn't the only department of the federal government that must operate according to the Constitution—there is also the executive, which includes not only the president but the many cabinet departments and agencies in his charge. And the states, too, are bound by the terms of the Constitution. While *Marbury* fit the early expectations about judicial review, as it involved an act of Congress, the institution has evolved, and federal courts are now asked to review regulatory and other actions by the executive as well as state laws and court decisions. Indeed, the far more common kind of judicial review today finds a court considering the constitutionality of some state action.

This volume contains illuminating discussions of specific exercises of judicial review by the Supreme Court over the past two centuries. The cases addressed by an outstanding group of scholars and practitioners include some of the most famous in constitutional law: the *Slaughter-House Cases* (1873), *Plessy* v. *Ferguson* (1896), *Adair* v. *United States* (1908), *Gitlow* v. *New York* (1925), and *Roe* v. *Wade* (1973).

These essays offer much to reflect upon. No reader can fail to be struck by the act of constitutional interpretation that is a part of judicial review. The framers of the Constitution did not advise judges how they should go about their task of interpretation, and they could hardly have imagined the variety of approaches that judges since *Marbury* have embraced. Through the years many of the Court's interpretations have proved controversial, to say the least. Consider *Dred Scott*, the 1857 decision holding that slaves were property protected by the Constitution—a ruling that helped precipitate the Civil War; or consider *Roe* v. *Wade*, the 1973 decision holding that the Constitution protects a woman's right to an abortion—a ruling that marks a battle line in today's culture wars.

The authors of these essays focus attention, in a given case, both on how the justices went about the task of constitutional interpretation and on alternative ways in which they *could* or *should* have gone about it. This task, and all that it involves, deserves the reflection of a citizenry that, for better or worse, has acquired the habit of translating its political disagreements into constitutional claims.

Preface

TERRY EASTLAND

This is a book about how judges—namely Supreme Court justices —have gone about the task of interpreting the Constitution. The cases discussed are among the best known in American constitutional law; several have figured prominently in debates over the confirmation of recent Supreme Court nominees.

The theorists at the American founding tended to see the Constitution as a body of fixed political principles, and they regarded its interpretation by judges as a relatively straightforward matter. What worried them were legislative bodies, thought to be the principal source of illiberal, not to say tyrannical, tendencies. The judicial department established by Article III thus represented an effort to ensure that Congress would be true to the Constitution, "the supreme law of the land." Those who framed and ratified the Constitution expected the judiciary to be, in the famous words of Alexander Hamilton, "the least dangerous branch" of government. From this notion of the benign judiciary there has from time to time (and especially in our own time) been dissent, even sharp dissent. The judicial labor of interpreting our fundamental law has proved to be more complex and controversial than its theorists and framers imagined.

In his essay treating the Court's approach to constitutional interpretation in its first decades, Walter Berns of the American Enterprise Institute mentions the Court's first great constitutional case, *Chisholm v. Georgia* (1793). A South Carolinian sued the state of Georgia. Georgia claimed immunity from the suit as a sovereign state and said the federal judiciary had no jurisdiction. Citing Article III's extension of the judicial power to "controversies . . . between a state and citizens of another state," the Supreme Court disagreed. *Chisholm* stirred antifederalist fears and led to the adoption, in 1798, of the Eleventh Amendment, which restricts the power of federal courts to hear suits against states brought by citizens of other states or aliens. While hardly divisive and threatening to the life of the nation, *Chisholm* illustrates how the people may respond to a constitutional decision they disagree with. However, the amendment process spelled out in Article V has been used only infrequently—perhaps seven times, depending on how one counts—as a means of overturning or correcting the Court's constitutional decisions.

Is there any other way to overrule the Court? As our history shows, the answer is yes—a future Court can do so. The Court sometimes changes or qualifies its mind not only on constitutional matters but on other ones as well. The fact that it does so highlights the importance of intelligently discussing and debating the Court's rulings and the doctrines by which it rules.

Another early case mentioned by Walter Berns is *Calder v. Bull* (1798), which casts a long forward shadow. The facts of the case—in which a state action was challenged as a violation of Article I's ban on *ex post facto* laws—need not delay us here. What made the case famous was the exchange between two justices who agreed on the result but appeared to disagree strenuously on how a judge should approach the task of constitutional interpretation. Justice Samuel Chase wrote: "There are certain vital principles in our free republican governments, which will determine and overrule an apparent and flagrant abuse of legislative power. . . . An act of the legislature (for I cannot call it a law), contrary to the great first principles of the social compact, cannot be considered a rightful exercise of legislative authority." Chase offered these examples of such "flagrant abuses": "a law that makes a man a judge in his own cause; or a law that takes property from A. and gives it to B." Chase appeared to be saying that the judiciary has authority to invalidate a law on grounds that it offends principles of "the social compact" (i.e., natural justice) regardless of whether those principles are stated in or can be fairly inferred from the Constitution. Justice James Iredell objected. The courts may not nullify a law "merely because it is, in their judgment, contrary to the principles of natural justice," he wrote; to do that would be contrary to our inherited (from England) legal tradition and to the very idea of a written constitution.

Chase and Iredell thus joined a debate over constitutional interpretation that has continued throughout our history. One finds echoes of Chase's position in Chief Justice John Marshall's opinion for the Court in *Fletcher* v. *Peck* (1810), in which he seemed to offer, as an alternative ground for the holding, "general principles, which are common to our free institutions." More clearly echoing Chase in the same case was Justice William Johnson, who declared that "general principle, on the reason and nature of things," justified the result. A slightly later opinion also cited by Berns is that of Justice Bushrod Washington in the circuit court case of *Corfield* v. *Coryell* (1823). Defining the "privileges and immunities of citizens" guaranteed by Article IV, Washington said they are "in their nature, fundamental" and "belong, of right, to the citizens of all free governments."

Berns contends, in effect, that Chase and Johnson and Washington are alive and well whenever the Court exercises what he calls its "natural justice jurisdiction." Members of the Court have seldom been so willing (or candid) as Chase was in *Calder* v. *Bull* to advance "natural justice" arguments not tied to some part of the Constitution. As Berns observes, justices who engage in natural-justice reasoning typically try to attach it to one bit of constitutional text or another, chiefly the Due Process Clause of the Fifth Amendment (which forbids the federal government to deprive any person of "life, liberty, or property without due process of law"); the Due Process Clause of the Fourteenth Amendment (which uses the same language to constrain the states); the Equal Protection Clause of the Fourteenth Amendment; and, in a quite recent develoment, the Ninth Amendment.

Of these, the Due Process Clauses have enjoyed the fullest employment by the Court. "Due process" originally referred to procedures that protect individuals from arbitrary treatment by government —the right to be protected against a warrantless arrest, the right to counsel, the right of the accused to know the nature of the evidence against him, and the like. But in the hands of the justices, due process also came to have a "substantive" meaning: there were certain things that government could not do, regardless of the justness of the procedures by which it might do them. The first justice to pour "substance" into the Fourteenth Amendment's Due Process Clause was Stephen J. Field, in his dissent in the *Slaughter-House Cases* (1873). Field declared that the clause protected certain liberties—among them "the right to pursue a lawful employment in a lawful manner, without other restraint than such as equally affects all persons." In Field's view, no state could enact a law that would interfere with that right.

By the end of the nineteenth century, the Court had begun to employ substantive due process to protect liberty of contract against abridgment by government, both state and federal. Perhaps the best known of its early substantive-due-process cases—mentioned often in the essays in this book—is *Lochner v. New York* (1905), in which the Court invalidated a New York statute limiting the number of hours a bakery employee could work in a week. The plaintiff succeeded in persuading the Court that the New York law violated his liberty of contract, guaranteed by the Fourteenth Amendment's Due Process Clause.

Three decades later the Court quit using the Due Process Clauses to protect liberty of contract and related notions of economic freedom. But, as Berns writes, the Court did not also quit exercising its "natural justice jurisdiction." The path-breaking case was *Griswold v. Connecticut* (1965), in which the Court held unconstitutional a state law criminalizing the use of contraceptives. To strike down this law, the Court had to find it violative of a constitutional right—what it called the right of privacy. The Court's opinion, written by Justice William O. Douglas and vigorously protested by Justice Hugo Black in dissent, declared that this right "emanated from" several constitutional guarantees found in the First, Third, Fourth, and Fifth amendments. Douglas himself abjured the doctrine of "substantive due process," as he understood it to refer to the line of economic-rights decisions dating to *Lochner.* But a good case can be made that Douglas created a new substantive due process, inasmuch as the right of privacy he declared entitled to constitutional protection seems tantamount to "liberty," which is explicitly mentioned in the Due Process Clauses of the Fifth and Fourteenth Amendments.

Be that as it may, *Griswold* prepared the way for the most controversial ruling in modern times, *Roe v. Wade* (1973). There the Court held that the right of privacy encompassed a woman's right to an abortion. *Roe* not only aroused a determined political movement but generated much heated discussion in both legal and political circles about its constitutional grounding; the reasoning in the opinion for the Court, written by Justice Harry Blackmun, has few defenders anywhere. (In her essay on *Roe* in this volume, Nadine Strossen, who advocates a broad interpretation of constitutional rights, remarks that Blackmun's opinion treated the constitutional basis of the decision "in a fairly offhanded fashion.") Asked several times to overrule *Roe,* the Supreme Court finally, in the 1992 case *Planned Parenthood* v. *Casey,* declined to do so. Instead the Court affirmed what the authors of an unusual "joint opinion" called "the essential holding" of *Roe* v. *Wade.*

By no means do all the contributors to this volume take issue with the results reached by the Supreme Court in the cases they discuss. Hadley Arkes of Amherst College examines two *Lochner*-era decisions involving labor unions that are usually classified as (old) substantive-due-process cases—*Adair* v. *United States* (1908) and *Coppage* v. *Kansas* (1915). Arkes contends that these decisions are properly rooted in, as he puts it, "the premises of personal freedom, with the notion that the worker, or the person, was the owner of himself, with the prime authority to commit his own labor." This freedom, he writes, depends on "a structure of privacy" that "marks off, unambiguously, a domain of private association." As he makes clear, this structure of privacy does not protect abortion. The domain of privacy, he says, is "the domain of the innocent, the legitimate, and the morally indifferent" —things abortion is not.

Nadine Strossen of New York Law School, who is president of the American Civil Liberties Union, advances a quite different view of privacy. In her essay on *Griswold, Roe,* and the doctrinally related case *Bowers* v. *Hardwick* (1986), she views privacy as encompassing "the right of individuals to make certain personal choices in the realm of sexual relationships, familial relationships, and childbearing." Strossen argues that because the Constitution "is designed to preserve individual liberty," the "liberty-protecting language" in the document "should be read at a high level of generality, to protect the most expansive conception of freedom." Interestingly, Strossen expresses doubt about the Court's effort to distinguish between property rights and personal rights.

Both Walter Berns and Charles Lofgren invite reflection on the Court's decision in the *Slaughter-House Cases* (1873). Berns contends that in sharply limiting the meaning of the Privileges or Immunities Clause of the Fourteenth Amendment, the Court got it wrong. Lofgren, in his extended treatment of *Slaughter-House,* agrees. "The dissenters," he writes, "had the better historically based constitutional argument," because the clause "was intended to protect a meaningful range of fundamental rights." Having virtually read the clause out of the Constitution a mere five years after the adoption of the Fourteenth Amendment, the Court eventually found itself using the Due Process and Equal Protection clauses to do what the Privileges or Immunities Clause, as originally understood, authorized it to do. Lofgren raises the fascinating question of what might have happened had the Court decided *Slaughter-House* differently by enforcing the Privileges or Immunities Clause. He suggests that "the clause, with its tangible guarantees," might have proved "less malleable clay in the hands of future judges than the two other clauses."

One of the most significant developments in modern constitutional law is the Court's application to the states of certain provisions in the Bill of Rights. As Akhil Amar of the Yale Law School reminds us in his essay, the Constitution, as interpreted by the Supreme Court in *Barron* v. *Baltimore* (1835), did not require states to respect the rights guaranteed by the first eight amendments of the Bill of Rights, which forbid only *Congress* to abridge those rights. Relying on the Fourteenth Amendment, the Supreme Court early in this century began the process of "incorporating" certain guarantees in the Bill of Rights as limitations upon the states also. The Court has seldom spent much time justifying incorporation in terms of constitutional text, history, or structure. As Amar says, incorporation has been adopted without "a lot of elaboration or justification." Amar undertakes to supply the needed justification, offering "not just a moral argument or an argument from justice" but a structural argument "about the foundation of our constitutional system."

The theme of the importance of arguments based on the structure of the Constitution is taken up by Mary Ann Glendon of the Harvard Law School in her essay, "Toward a Structural Approach to Constitutional Interpretation." She commends the efforts of a growing group of legal scholars who are "approaching interpretive problems by attending to the overall design of the Constitution and the mutually conditioning relationships among its provisions."

Where are we now, on this sometimes slippery slope of constitutional interpretation? Gerard V. Bradley of the Notre Dame Law School advances the provocative argument that the Supreme Court has traded in the historic Constitution for a new one. Bradley focuses on two cases from the 1991-92 term: *Planned Parenthood* v. *Casey*, in which the Court affirmed that abortion is a fundamental constitutional right, and *Lee* v. *Weisman*, in which the Court declared that the inclusion of a prayer at a public school graduation ceremony violated the ban on the establishment of religion found in the First Amendment. Bradley contends that *Casey* and *Lee* constitute "the summation of a comprehensive judicial project, dating almost entirely from World War II and mostly from 1960." In this project, the Court's decisions are justified not really by the Constitution but by what Bradley calls "the rational approach of a theory of the human person and a normative view of the judicial function in a pluralistic democracy."

If Bradley is right, those who framed and ratified the Constitution would be astonished at what judges have done, through the power of interpretation, to the supreme law of the land. Yet one does not have to agree with Bradley to believe that how the Supreme Court interprets the Constitution should be a subject of abiding interest, if not concern, to the American people. By focusing on some of the Court's great constitutional cases and controversies, *Benchmarks* aims to stimulate reflection about the most important work of the nation's highest Court.

Acknowledgments

Most of the essays in *Benchmarks* originated at a conference sponsored by the Ethics and Public Policy Center and held in Washington, D.C., in June 1992. The essay by Gerard V. Bradley grew out a paper he presented elsewhere, a part of which was published in *The World & I*.

An Appendix that begins on page 151 gives the texts of most of the parts of the Constitution to which the essayists refer.

The editing of the essays was done by Carol Griffith, senior editor at the Ethics and Public Policy Center. Staff members Marianne Geers and Eric Owens helped with the manuscript preparation.

The editor of the volume is grateful to the seven contributors, to Griffin B. Bell for the foreword, and to his staff colleagues who brought this book to fruition.

1

Constitutional Interpretation in the Court's First Decades

WALTER BERNS

The Supreme Court decided no cases whatever in its first three years—1789, when the first justices were appointed, through 1791—and in the years immediately following it decided very few cases of great national import. In this early period, most cases that came to the Court involved maritime law or were disputes between a state and either citizens of another state or citizens or subjects of a foreign state. Such cases as these were not likely to involve issues of broader interest. A few early cases—examples are *Chisholm* v. *Georgia* in 1793, and *Ware* v. *Hylton* in 1796—were nationally important, constitutionally important, cases; the decision in *Chisholm,* for example, gave rise to a constitutional amendment depriving federal courts of their jurisdiction in cases like it. But who remembers, or today has reason to read, *Glass* v. *The Sloop Betsy* (1794), *Bingham* v. *Cabbott* (1795), or *Pennhallow* v. *Doane* (1795)?

Yet the early justices seem to have been keenly aware that they were laying the foundation on which future judges, as well as legislators

Walter Berns is a resident scholar at the American Enterprise Institute and an emeritus professor of government at Georgetown University. His most recent book is *Taking the Constitution Seriously* (1987).

and executives, would have to build a nation, and their cases are worth reading, not so much for the judgments reached as for what is said in the course of reaching them. This is nowhere clearer than in Justice William Patterson's opinion in *Van Horne's Lessee* v. *Dorrance,* a case decided in 1795 in the U.S. circuit court in Pennsylvania. In England, said Patterson, Parliament is supreme; its authority "runs without limits, and rises above control." But in America the case is very different: "Every State in the Union has its constitution reduced to written exactitude and precision." What is a constitution? "It is the form of government, delineated by the mighty hand of the people, in which certain first principles of fundamental laws are established. The Constitution is certain and fixed; it contains the permanent will of the people [and is] not to be worked upon by the temper of the times, nor to rise and fall with the tide of events."[1]

Some of the early cases are worth reading for what was said in the oral arguments. For example, in *Ware* v. *Hylton* we find John Marshall, in his only appearance as counsel before the Court, saying that "the judicial authority can have no right to question the validity of a law unless such a jurisdiction is expressly given by the Constitution" (a statement that, to say the least, does not prepare us for what Marshall was to do later in *Marbury* v. *Madison*). And if such jurisdiction *is* given in the Constitution, the judiciary's role is to enforce the written provisions of the law, not, as Marshall put it, "the laws of God." An act of the government, even "though disgraceful," he said, "would be obligatory on the judiciary department."[2] Some matters belong to the legislature, not to the judiciary. As Justice Felix Frankfurter was to say many years later, "we do not sit like a kadi under a tree dispensing justice according to considerations of individual expediency."[3]

In *Hepburn and Dundas* v. *Ellzey* (1804), the Court had to decide whether the circuit court had jurisdiction to hear a suit brought by a citizen in the District of Columbia against a citizen of Virginia. The issue turned on whether, in the law dealing with diversity jurisdiction, Congress intended the District to be treated as if it were a state. The Court, with Marshall, now chief justice, writing the opinion, said that "the act of Congress obviously uses the word 'state' in reference to that term as used in the constitution" and, after examining the various clauses in which the term appears, determined that the term could not be understood to include the District of Columbia. The denial of jurisdiction followed as a matter of course, but not as a matter of judicial preference. "It is true," Marshall said, "that as citizens of the United States, and of that particular district which is subject to the jurisdiction of Congress it is extraordinary that the courts of the United States, which are open to aliens, and to the citizens of every state in the union, should be closed upon them. But this is a subject for legislation, not for judicial consideration."[4] (Surprisingly, Congress did not get around to adopting such legislation until 1940.)

Marshall and the Rights of Nature

To return to *Ware* v. *Hylton:* we also find Marshall as counsel referring to "the state of nature." This tells us something about where he was coming from, as we say today, as well as where he would go later when he was on the Court. We can expect someone who speaks of the state of nature to be familiar with the *rights* of nature, and to repair to them in his judicial opinions when it is appropriate to do so.

So it was in an 1825 admiralty case, *The Antelope,* where Chief Justice Marshall speaks of "the sacred rights of liberty and property." Unfortunately, these rights were in conflict in this case, because the property involved was a number of captured slaves. The Court, with Marshall writing the opinion, felt obliged to recognize that international law did not regard the slave trade as piracy. That meant, in this case, that certain (but not all) of the claimants were entitled to their property. But the slave trade was criminal under the laws of the United States and, moreover, "inhuman" according to the laws of nature. To the extent that it could (international law being as it was), the Court took cognizance of this in its order disposing of the slaves among the various claimants. The Portuguese got none because "no subject of the crown of Portugal has appeared to assert his title to this property," Marshall said. "This inattention to a subject of so much real interest . . . is so contrary to the common course of human action as to justify serious suspicion that the real owner [of the slaves] dares not avow himself."[5] The implication is, of course, that, in his embarrassment, the Portuguese claimant shared the Court's opinion as to the inhumanity of the slave trade.

Marshall's recognition of the rights of nature, or of the origin of rights in nature, was even more evident in his minority opinion in

Ogden v. *Saunders* (1827). "In the state of nature," he said, "individuals may contract, their contracts are obligatory, and force may rightfully be employed to coerce the party who has broken his engagement." He then went on to consider the effect of society upon those rights: "When men unite together and form a government, do they surrender their right to contract, as well as their right to enforce the observance of contracts? For what purpose should they make this surrender?" His conclusion was, of course, that the surrender had never been made. "These rights," he said, "are not given by society, but are brought into it. The right of coercion is necessarily surrendered to government, and this surrender imposes on government the correlative duty of furnishing a remedy."[6]

As Patterson said in the case of *Van Horne's Lessee,* the right of acquiring and possessing property and having it protected is "one of the natural, inherent, and unalienable rights of man. . . . The preservation of property then is a primary object of the social compact."[7] The same judgment informed the opinions in the great cases decided by the Marshall court, such as *Fletcher* v. *Peck, McCulloch* v. *Maryland, Dartmouth College* v. *Woodward,* and *Osborn* v. *Bank of the United States.*

From these early cases we derive the following general principles: constitutional, not legislative, supremacy; constitutional, not judicial, supremacy; the immutability of the written constitution (a point driven home by Marshall in *Marbury* v. *Madison*); and national, not state, supremacy. What requires further discussion is the place of natural right or natural law in the written constitution.

The Early Justices and Natural Law

Marshall followed the passage in *Ogden* v. *Saunders* on the natural character of the right to contract with the assertion that "this reasoning is, undoubtedly, much strengthened by the authority of those writers on natural and national law, whose opinions have been viewed with profound respect by the wisest men of the present and past ages."[8] Although he did not identify the "writers" he had in mind, his references to the state of nature and his emphasis on the property right suggest that he could only have meant John Locke and his followers.

But Marshall's use of the term "natural law" has given rise to the opinion, held by some writers today, that he and his colleagues on the early Court understood the Constitution to be informed by the principles of natural law as taught by Cicero and later by Thomas Aquinas. The conclusion these modern writers draw is that, when expounding the Constitution, the justices might properly appeal to natural law or natural justice. This is a mistaken conclusion.

True, the records of the nation's founding period are not devoid of references of this sort. In his celebrated law lectures of 1791, Justice James Wilson, having said that parliament "may, unquestionably, be controlled by natural or revealed law, proceeding from *divine* authority," went on to say that in the United States "the legislative authority is subjected to another control, beside that arising from natural or revealed law; it is subjected to the control arising from the constitution."[9] This might be taken to mean *in addition to* natural or revealed law, except that in the sequel Wilson makes it evident that he meant no such thing.

No such ambiguity can be found in William Rawle's *View of the Constitution of the United States* (1825). Rawle was a loyalist who studied law at the Middle Temple, London, returned to Philadelphia after the Revolution, and in the years 1791-99 served as U.S. attorney for Pennsylvania. Briefly, his thesis is this: there is law prior to the formation of civil society; this law, "emphatically termed the law of nature, [is] implanted in us by nature itself"; this law became part of the common law; the common law provides rules of decision in certain state cases; in some circumstances (e.g., in diversity cases), the judicial power of the United States extends to those cases because they are cases "arising under [the] Constitution" of the United States; therefore, federal courts have a natural-law jurisdiction, or, to put this differently, this unwritten natural law provides rules of decision in some federal cases.[10]

What enabled Rawle to accept this conclusion so readily was his confidence that knowledge of the natural law required no learning or study; it is "felt," he said, and "never misunderstood." James Madison did not share that confidence, to say the least. The precise extent of the common law, he wrote in *Federalist* 37, remains still to be clearly and finally established in Great Britain, where accuracy in such subjects has been more industriously pursued than in other parts of the world. "The jurisdiction of her several courts, general and local, of law, of equity, or admiralty, etc., is not less a source of frequent and intricate discussions, sufficiently denoting the indeterminate limits by which they are respectively circumscribed."

But Madison's principal objection to the common law had to do with its unrepublican character. George Mason had complained that the common law was not secured by the Constitution, and Madison wondered what the Framers might have done to secure it:

> If they had in general terms declared the Common Law to be in force, they would have broken in upon the legal Code of every State in the most material points; they wd. have done more, they would have brought over from G[reat] B[ritain] a thousand heterogeneous & antirepublican doctrines, and even the *ecclesiastical Hierarchy itself,* for that is part of the Common law [and if] they had undertaken a discrimination [as some of the states had done], they would have formed a digest of laws, instead of a Constitution.[11]

And what he said about the common law, with or without a natural-law substance, can be said emphatically about the natural law as it was understood prior to the discovery of the rights of man and the founding of the United States: it rested on principles foreign and antithetical to those of the Declaration of Independence. For example, according to pre-modern natural law, as opposed to the Declaration of Independence, men are *not* naturally endowed with the right to pursue happiness as they themselves define it, and therefore the separation of church and state is an infraction of that law. According to pre-modern natural law, church and state are one, or the state performs the function of a church; it prescribes the *ends* of human life, and by doing so defines the happiness men are to pursue. This is made clear by Thomas Aquinas, the principal expositor of that law.

For Aquinas, who made Cicero's doctrine, with modifications, a part of the Western tradition, the natural law is grounded in the eternal law—which is to say, in God himself, or in his providence or governance. It derives its strength ultimately from the threat of divine punishment but immediately (and necessarily) from the more evident threat of civil punishment. While the principles of the natural law are promulgated and known to all men (insofar as they are rational), those principles alone do not serve as a sufficient guide for human actions. This means that the natural law has to be supplemented by human law, which, modeled on the natural law, provides a surer guide to virtuous action. Besides, men are not equally disposed to follow the path described by the law; their actions have to be commanded or prohibited under the threat of punishment prescribed by the human law.

In the strict sense, men have to be ruled—ruled, as Aquinas says, by "a few wise men competent to frame right laws."[12] Government framed on this model derives its just powers from God, not from the consent of the governed—which is to say, it is incompatible with the principles of the Constitution of the United States.

The Appeal to "Natural Justice"

There is no denying the temptation to appeal to the natural law, and on at least one early occasion a Supreme Court justice succumbed to the temptation. The case was *Calder* v. *Bull* (1798), where the Court held that an act of the Connecticut legislature setting aside a probate-court decree was not an *ex post facto* law and, therefore, was not void under Article I, Section 10, of the Constitution. Having delivered that judgment, Justice Samuel Chase, in what can only be described as *dicta*, went on to say that state authority is limited not only by express constitutional prohibitions but also by the "first principles of the social compact."

For this, Chase was taken to task by his colleague Justice James Iredell. "It is true," said Iredell, "that some speculative jurists have held, that a legislative act against natural justice must, in itself, be void; but I cannot think that, under such a government, any court of justice would possess a power to declare it so." The ideas of natural justice, he continued, "are regulated by no fixed standard. . . ."[13] There is little question that on this point Iredell was expressing the view of the Framers, and that they held this view largely for the reasons he gave.

True, on one occasion, Marshall seemingly acknowledged the right of the Supreme Court to appeal to something akin to "natural justice." Announcing the judgment of the Court in the politically explosive case of *Fletcher* v. *Peck,* he said that "the state of Georgia was restrained [from passing the law in question] either by general principles, which are common to our free institutions, or by the particular provisions of the Constitution of the United States"; this, he said, was "the unanimous opinion of the court." But in writing his opinion, Marshall himself relied solely on an express provision of the Constitution: the Georgia law, he said, was one "impairing the obligations of Contracts" in violation of Article I, Section 10.

It was Justice William Johnson who had recourse to the idea of natural justice. "I do not hesitate to declare," he said in a concurring opinion, "that a state does not possess the power of revoking its own grants," but, he added, "I do it on a general principle, on the reason and nature of things: a principle which will impose laws even on the Deity."[14] It would appear that Marshall felt compelled by the political situation to announce a judgment that had the support of a "unanimous" Court, and that this necessity led him to speak of "general principles" in addition to an express constitutional provision.

Honoring the Written Text

Put simply, the idea that the judges are entitled to rest their decisions on the principles of "natural justice" is incompatible with the Framers' idea of a written constitution. With a written text, they held, comes certainty, and with certainty comes legitimacy; and both certainty and legitimacy are put in jeopardy by rules of constitutional construction that, in effect, permit the judges to do as they will. Madison even had reason to complain (albeit mildly) of Marshall's opinion for the Court in the *McCulloch* case:

> But [he said] it was anticipated . . . by few if any of the friends of the Constitution, that a rule of construction would be introduced as broad & as pliant as what has occurred. And those who recollect, and still more those who shared in what passed in the State Conventions, thro' which the people ratified the Constitution . . . cannot easily be persuaded that the avowal of such a rule would not have prevented its ratification. . . .
>
> There is certainly a reasonable medium between expounding the Constitution with the strictness of a penal law, or other ordinary statute, and expounding it with a laxity which may vary its essential character, and encroach on the local sovereignties with which it was meant to be reconcilable.[15]

If, as he said in a subsequent letter, the judges are not guided by the sense of the people who ratified the Constitution, "there can be no security for a consistent and stable, more than for a *faithful,* exercise of its powers."[16] The legitimacy of government depends on adherence to the written text, the text the people ratified; so, too, does the possibility of limited or constitutional government.

The classic statement of these propositions can be found in Marshall's opinion for the Court in *Marbury* v. *Madison.* He said the "whole American fabric has been erected" on the principle that government derives from and is dependent on the will of the people. "This original and supreme will organizes the government, and assigns to different departments their respective powers"; in the American case, it also assigns limits to those powers; "and that those limits may not be mistaken or forgotten, the constitution is written." It was for this reason that he (and, he suggested, all Americans) deemed a written constitution to be "the greatest improvement on political institutions."[17] Thomas Jefferson made the same point when he said that "the possession of a written Constitution [is America's] peculiar security."[18]

But did not the great chief justice himself also enjoin us never to forget that this Constitution is one "intended to endure for ages to come, and consequently, to be adapted to the various crises of human affairs"? And what is this but a declaration that its vitality or viability depends on its adaptability, which, in turn, depends on the willingness of the justices to appeal to principles outside the text—for example, to something that might be designated the principles of natural justice?

The words are indeed Marshall's, but, as I have often pointed out, they are strung together from passages separated by some eight pages in the Supreme Court reports.[19] Chief Justice Charles Evans Hughes was the first to string them together, in a 1934 opinion,[20] and in this form they have been repeated on countless occasions by others. Marshall did not say the Constitution may be adapted to the "various crises of human affairs"; he said the legislative powers granted by the Constitution are adaptable to meet those crises. And much of what we regard as the inevitability of judicial activism is the result of Congress's failure to use its legislative powers under Section Five of the Fourteenth Amendment. This failure—specifically, the failure to declare that one of the "privileges or immunities" of American citizenship is to attend a nonsegregated public school—opened the door for the Court; and, as we say, the rest is history.

Justice Washington's Mistake

For this we can blame one of Marshall's colleagues, Justice Bushrod Washington, and his opinion for the circuit court in *Corfield* v. *Coryell* (1823). *Corfield* was a trespass action brought against a resident of Delaware under a law of the state of New Jersey forbidding non-residents "to take or gather . . . oysters . . . in any of the rivers, bays, or waters in [that] state, on board [any] vessel not wholly owned" by a New Jersey resident. *Corfield* offered a defense based, in part, on Article IV, Section 2, #1 of the Constitution: "The citizens of each state shall be entitled to all privileges and immunities of citizens in the several states."

Justice Washington asked, What are privileges and immunities? and answered: They are those privileges and immunities "which are, in their nature, fundamental [and] which belong, of right, to the citizens of all free governments."[21] As such, they would be identified and defined by the courts. The question he *should* have asked is, What are *these* privileges and immunities? And he should have answered, They are the attributes of state citizenship and, as such, were to be defined by each state. Like the equivalent clause in the Articles of Confederation (Article IV), the constitutional clause was intended to prevent the states from discriminating against citizens of the United States resident in other states.

Justice Washington's misreading of the clause was to have far-reaching consequences; it led the Supreme Court to misinterpret the Privileges or Immunities Clause of the Fourteenth Amendment. That amendment, of course, contains a provision similar to that in Article IV, except that it speaks of "the privileges or immunities of *citizens of the United States,*" and forbids the states to make or enforce any law abridging them. If, on a proper reading of the Article IV provision, the privileges and immunities of "citizens in the several states" were to be defined in the constitutions and laws of the several states, it would seem to follow that "the privileges or immunities of citizens of the United States" were to be defined in the Constitution and laws of the United States. In a word, having been forbidden to discriminate against citizens resident in other states, the states were now forbidden to discriminate against their own residents who were citizens of the United States. And what constituted discrimination would be defined by Congress. This reading is strengthened by Section 5 of the Fourteenth Amendment, which gives Congress the "power to enforce, by appropriate legislation, the provisions of this article."

Justice Samuel F. Miller, speaking for the Court in the *Slaughter-House Cases* (1873), rejected this conclusion as unthinkable.[22] The authors of the Fourteenth Amendment, he said, did not intend "to bring within the power of Congress the entire domain of civil rights heretofore belonging exclusively to the states." What, then, are privileges or immunities? "They are, in the language of Judge Washington, those rights which are fundamental," and Miller proceeded to give a few examples, such as the right of a citizen to come to the seat of government to assert any claim he may have upon that government and the right of free access to its seaports. This had the effect of rendering the clause a "practical nullity," to quote the Annotated Constitution.[23]

How was it possible for Justice Miller to consider it "unthinkable" that the victors in the Civil War, when they amended the Constitution, had intended "radically [to change] the whole theory of the relations of the state and Federal governments to each other and of both these governments to the people"? Or, more precisely, why was it "unthinkable" that, "by the simple declaration that no State shall make or enforce any law which shall abridge the privileges or immunities of citizens of the United States," the authors of the Fourteenth Amendment had intended "to transfer the security and protection of civil rights from the States to the Federal government"? Still more to my point (and still quoting Miller's opinion in *Slaughter-House*), when authorizing Congress to enforce the provision by appropriate legislation, why was it "unthinkable" that the authors of the amendment had intended that Congress might, quite properly, "pass laws in advance, limiting and restricting the legislative power by the States"? Whatever Miller's reasons, the powers he denied to Congress are, in large part, now being exercised by the Supreme Court as part of their "natural justice" jurisdiction.

The instrument employed by the Court is the Due Process Clause, whose language, even when given a "substantive" form, is not suited to the many uses to which it has been put; or the Equal Protection Clause; or more recently, the Fourteenth Amendment in general and the Ninth Amendment (the Enumeration Clause). Here, for example, is Justice Harry Blackmun speaking for the Court in *Roe* v. *Wade,* the abortion case: "This right to privacy, whether it be founded in the Fourteenth Amendment's concept of personal liberty . . . or, as the District Court determined, in the Ninth Amendment's reservation of rights to the people, is broad enough to encompass a woman's decision whether or not to terminate her pregnancy."[24] The Fourteenth or the Ninth, and, like the heroine in Gilbert and Sullivan's *Iolanthe,* he didn't care which.

And, as Justice Blackmun indicated in his dissent in the Georgia homosexual sodomy case,[25] it is the job of the Court to identify fundamental rights and, having done so, find a place for them in the Constitution. The preferred place is the Ninth Amendment, the most commodious, with room for all those newly discovered "natural laws." As that onetime doyen of the law fraternity Roscoe Pound put it, "Unlike the law of nature of the eighteenth century the revived natural law is not a fixed system of precisely formulated rules to stand fast forever." This can only mean, if it means anything, that while nature presumably stays the same, its laws change with the times. The same is true with natural rights: "From this standpoint [Pound writes] the Ninth Amendment is a solemn declaration that natural rights are not a fixed category of reasonable human expectation . . . laid down once for all in the several sections of the Constitution."[26] Which means that the Constitution changes with the times, a flat contradiction of what the Framers and early Supreme Court justices had to say on the subject.

The man indirectly responsible for this heretical view was Bushrod Washington, one of those early justices.

2

Interpreting the Fourteenth Amendment: Approaches in *Slaughter-House* and *Plessy*

CHARLES A. LOFGREN

AMENDMENT 14, Section 1. All persons born or naturalized in the United States, and subject to the jurisdiction thereof, are citizens of the United States and of the State wherein they reside. No State shall make or enforce any law which shall abridge the privileges or immunities of citizens of the United States; nor shall any State deprive any person of life, liberty, or property, without due process of law; nor deny to any person within its jurisdiction the equal protection of the laws.

Among the early interpretations of the Fourteenth Amendment were those advanced in the *Slaughter-House Cases* (1873)[1] and *Plessy v. Ferguson* (1896).[2] In *Slaughter-House*, the Supreme Court grappled with the amendment for the first time (although individual justices had already confronted it on circuit). *Plessy* by no means marked the Court's initial foray into the amendment's application to

---

Charles A. Lofgren is the Roy P. Crocker Professor of American History and Politics at Claremont McKenna College and also a member of the Graduate Faculty in History of the Claremont Colleges. He is the author of *The Plessy Case: A Legal-Historical Interpretation* (Oxford University Press, 1988).

race relations, but it was, as Professor David Currie has observed, "a reliable symbol of the times."[3]

The questions I shall take up in relation to these cases are: (1) What conclusions did the Court reach about the meaning of the Fourteenth Amendment? (2) What interpretive approaches did the justices take in reaching those conclusions? And (3) what difference might it have made if the dissenters in each case had prevailed? The last of these is the sort of question that we historians don't often ask, at least explicitly, but it is intriguing enough to warrant a bit of speculation.

Both *Slaughter-House* and *Plessy* involved the Thirteenth Amendment as well as the Fourteenth, but for the most part I will ignore this dimension and focus on the Fourteenth. The Thirteenth Amendment issues were less important.

THE SLAUGHTER-HOUSE CASES

In March 1869 the Louisiana legislature passed Act 118, which forbade slaughtering in New Orleans and the parishes of Orleans, Jefferson, and St. Bernard—an area of over 1,100 square miles—except within a specified area below the city. There the Crescent City Company was given an exclusive twenty-five-year grant to build and operate "a grand slaughterhouse of sufficient capacity to accommodate all butchers," along with livestock landing and holding facilities. Independent butchers using the slaughterhouse and other facilities were required to pay prescribed fees, and the company received the non-edible parts of any animals slaughtered by the independents.[4]

Corruption greased the passage of the law. Of the 20,000 shares of stock authorized by the act of incorporation, the seventeen incorporators promised 2,000 to three assistants to the state governor, to insure his approval—and were chagrined to learn that he had signed the bill without requiring the gift. Along the way, legislators had similarly received pledges of stock, along with interest-free loans. Later disputes among the incorporators led to litigation disclosing the inner workings of what one judge labeled "a wholesale bribery concern."[5]

While the sordid details of the company's creation have caught the attention of later commentators, other circumstances, too, are important in explaining the grant. For one thing, the monopoly appeared lucrative. New Orleans in the late 1860s seemed poised to become a major center for the slaughtering business. To the west, millions of cattle roamed the Texas plains, and plans for river improvements and railway construction promised a means for delivering the beasts to the city. To the north, markets awaited, made more accessible by techno-logical advances in refrigeration.[6] A second factor was the messy nature of the slaughtering business itself. The existing slaughterhouses in and near New Orleans had located along the Mississippi River within the city and then had moved *upstream* as the population grew. In 1867, one city health officer commented:

> The amount of filth thrown into the river above the source from which the city is supplied with water, and coming from the slaughterhouses[,] is incredible. Barrels filled with entrails, liver, blood, urine, dung, and other refuse, portions in an advanced stage of decomposition, are constantly being thrown into the river but a short distance from the banks, poisoning the air with offensive smells and necessarily contaminating the water near the banks for miles.[7]

An obvious solution was to restrict the location of facilities, but an additional expedient readily suggested itself—a monopoly grant. Con-temporary Paris offered the model of a monopoly that had been justified on grounds of public health, and so did several large American cities.

Not unexpectedly, when "the seventeen" received their grant, the independent butchers protested. They sought and obtained a prelimi-nary injunction against the Crescent City Company, whereupon Cres-cent City went into another district court and obtained an injunction against the butchers, enjoining them from interfering with the mo-nopoly. The independents nonetheless incorporated themselves as the Live Stock Dealers' and Butchers' Association and began planning their own facility below the city and its water supply. They also obtained an injunction from another district court against interference from the Crescent City monopoly. At that point the state attorney general obtained an injunction from yet another district court forbid-ding use of the independent butchers' facilities. Then the banker who had built the new facilities for the independent butchers obtained an order against the state and the Crescent City Company. All told, perhaps 200 suits were filed.

Opposing counsel eventually agreed on six suits to appeal to the state supreme court. In April 1870 that court upheld the Crescent City Company's exclusive grant, over the dissent of one member. Among other claims, the independent butchers' counsel—who included John A. Campbell, a former justice of the United States Supreme Court —had argued that Act 118 deprived their clients of rights under the Thirteenth and Fourteenth Amendments to the federal Constitution. The highest state court having denied federal claims, the butchers could take their cases to the U.S. Supreme Court on writ of error, which Associate Justice Joseph P. Bradley "allowed" (to use the statutory language) while holding circuit court in Galveston during May 1870. This constituted a stay on all previous orders and on further state proceedings.

But in March 1870 the Louisiana legislature had created another district court—the Eighth—"with exclusive jurisdiction to issue writs of injunction." The Crescent City Company now went into the new court and obtained a fresh order against the independent butchers, and using it the New Orleans police seized meat already on the way to market. At this point, the butchers asked Justice Bradley and Circuit Judge William B. Woods—then sitting together in New Orleans as the United States Circuit Court for the District of Louisiana—for an injunction against the Crescent City Company that would suspend *all* state proceedings against the butchers. Former justice Campbell argued for the butchers that the multitudinous actions by the state and through the state courts deprived the butchers of rights secured by the Civil Rights Act of 1866 and Section One of the Fourteenth Amendment. The company's answer was that the circuit court's jurisdiction did not extend to issuing orders to state courts, that the same issues were already before the U.S. Supreme Court on writ of error, and that Act 118 "contain[ed] only police regulations, in no manner conflicting with the constitution of the United States, or the amendments thereof."[8]

The circuit court decided for the butchers—up to a point—and Bradley wrote its opinion, which anticipated his later dissent when the U.S. Supreme Court decided *Slaughter-House.* The butchers' application brought up the question, he said,

whether the fourteenth amendment to the constitution is intended to secure to the citizens of the United States of all classes merely equal rights; or whether it is intended to secure to them any absolute rights. And, if the latter, whether the rights claimed by the [butchers] . . . are among the number of such absolute rights.[9]

Focusing on the amendment's Privileges or Immunities Clause, Bradley found that it conveyed absolute rights, which included the right "of every American citizen to adopt and follow such lawful industrial pursuit—not injurious to the community—as he may see fit, without unreasonable regulation or molestation. . . ." Such "privileges [could] not be invaded without sapping the very foundations of republican government[, which] . . . is not merely a government of the people, but . . . is a free government."[10]

As for the butchers' claim under the Civil Rights Act of 1866, Bradley at first concluded that the act did not apply; but after further reflection overnight, he modified his opinion. Although the measure did not enlarge on the rights covered by the Fourteenth Amendment, it provided "additional guarantees and remedies," he said.[11]

In the end, however, after ruling for the butchers on the merits of their claims and enjoining the Crescent City Company from interfering with their operations, Bradley excepted Crescent City's injunction obtained from Louisiana's Eighth Circuit Court. The problem was a provision of the jurisdictional statute that Bradley interpreted as forbidding stays against proceedings already commenced in state courts.[12]

This outcome, along with a decision by the U.S. Supreme Court that it lacked jurisdiction to stay the orders of the state district courts in New Orleans,[13] put the litigation into the form we know as the "Slaughter-House Cases." With the independent butchers unable to pursue their occupation, their corporation settled with the monopoly and agreed to end the litigation. On the basis of the settlement agreements, counsel for Crescent City asked the U.S. Supreme Court to dismiss the cases; but because some of the independents (members of the long-standing Butchers' Benevolent Association) had not joined in the agreements, adverse parties remained in the three cases eventually decided by the Court.[14]

The Supreme Court Decides

The United States Supreme Court's decision upholding Act 118 came down in April 1873. This followed a reargument necessitated by a four-to-four split after the cases were first argued in January 1872. In the meantime, Justice Samuel Nelson, who had missed the first argument because of ill health, had resigned and been replaced by Ward Hunt. The Court in fact postponed reargument until Hunt took his seat.

Throughout, both sides were well represented. With sweeping arguments about the revolutionary scope of both the Thirteenth and the Fourteenth Amendment, former justice Campbell clearly lived up to the adage "Leave it to God and Mr. Campbell." Walton Hamilton's classic article conveys the flavor of his presentation:

> In [Campbell's] briefs, there is nothing of clean-cut concept, of rule of law chiseled with neatness and precision, of sweep of syllogism to its inevitable therefore. . . . His endeavor is marked, not with the delicate articulation of the codifier, but by the daring of the adventurer and the fumbling of the pioneer. . . . He abandoned the older parts of the Constitution, whose well-litigated clauses did not point his way, and took his stand upon an article which as yet had drawn forth no judicial utterance.[15]

Campbell's co-counsel J. Q. A. Fellows surveyed the intent of the amendments and related legislation as disclosed in congressional debates.

On the other side, counsel for Crescent City denied the butchers' charge of monopoly by explaining how Act 118 allowed the independents to use the slaughterhouse facilities. They also stressed the sweep of the police power and the limited impact of the Reconstruction Amendments (amendments 13-15) on the federal system. Campbell's interpretation, they contended, would have the revolutionary consequence of "depriv[ing] the [state] legislatures and state courts . . . from regulating and settling their internal affairs."[16]

Justice Samuel Miller, speaking for the Court, largely accepted Crescent City's position. He denied that Act 118 deprived the independent butchers of their right to labor or pursue their business, and he interpreted the law's restrictions as falling within the police power already well established by legal authorities. Chancellor James Kent of New York, Chief Justice Lemuel Shaw of Massachusetts, Chief Justice Isaac F. Redfield of Vermont, and Chief Justice John Marshall were all drawn on in this regard. The only question was whether the new amendments narrowed the police power of the states.

Miller focused on the butchers' Fourteenth Amendment argument, particularly the claim that the right of following a lawful occupation was a "privilege or immunity" of citizens of the United States. Here he developed a crucial distinction. Without denying that the right in question existed, he argued that it was a right of state citizenship, not national citizenship, and hence not protected by the Privileges or Immunities Clause. This distinction he derived from juxtaposing the first clause of Section One—"All persons born or naturalized in the United States, and subject to the jurisdiction thereof, are citizens of the United States and of the state wherein they reside"—with the second clause, which only forbids state abridgment of the privileges or immunities of citizens of the *United States*. Justice Miller's reasoning was as follows:

> It is a little remarkable, if this clause was intended as a protection to the citizen of a state against the legislative power of his own state, that the words "citizen of the state" should be left out when it is [*sic*] so carefully used, and used in contradistinction to "citizens of the United States" in the very sentence which precedes it. It is too clear for argument that the change in phraseology was adopted understandingly and with a purpose.[17]

He went on to explain that to adopt the opposite conclusion—that the Privileges or Immunities Clause brought the rights of both state and U.S. citizenship under federal protection—would work a revolution in federal-state relations that surely the nation had never intended in adopting the amendment.[18]

The Due Process and Equal Protection clauses received scant attention. Indeed, Miller remarked that argument drawing on them "has not been much pressed in these cases."[19]

The Dissents

Four members of the Court dissented—Chief Justice Chase and Justices Field, Bradley, and Swayne—and all but Chase filed opinions. Scholars have disagreed on which of the dissenting opinions staked out the most radical position. In the main, however, their arguments were complementary; and both Bradley and Swayne (along with the chief justice) concurred in Field's dissent.

Justice Stephen J. Field tore into Miller's Fourteenth Amendment argument, particularly his conclusion about the rights attaching to state versus national citizenship. Section One's Citizenship Clause, Field explained, was not designed to create two categories of citizenship with respect to the protection of privileges or immunities, but rather to clarify the relationship between state and national citizenship and to overturn the conclusion in the *Dred Scott* case that blacks could not be citizens. As Field understood the clause, it "change[d] the whole subject [of citizenship], and remove[d] it from the region of discussion and doubt." U.S. citizenship was now primary, and "[a] citizen of a state . . . [was] only a citizen of the United States residing in that state." With this new locus of citizenship came new protections. "The fundamental rights, privileges, and immunities which belong to [a person] as a free man and a free citizen, now belong to him as a citizen of the United States, and are not dependent upon his citizenship in any state." If, as the majority held, the Privileges or Immunities Clause primarily gave federal protection only to rights *already* cloaked with federal protection against state infringement, "it was a vain and idle enactment, which accomplished nothing, and most unnecessarily excited Congress and the people on its passage."[20]

Field then examined authorities and found that among the extensive rights protected by the Privileges or Immunities Clause was the pursuit of a lawful occupation. Police regulations, which "[t]he state may prescribe . . . for every pursuit and calling of life as will promote the public health, secure the good order and advance the prosperity of society," were legitimate only when they encompassed restrictions "imposed equally upon all others of the same age, sex, and condition." "[G]rants of exclusive privileges, such as are made by the act in question," he concluded, "are opposed to the whole theory of free government, and it requires no bill of rights to render them void. That only is a free government, in the American sense of the term, under which the inalienable right of every citizen to pursue his happiness is unrestrained, except by just, equal, and impartial laws."[21]

Justice Joseph P. Bradley in his dissent amplified Field's argument with respect to both the content of the rights protected by the Privileges or Immunities Clause and the unreasonableness of the monopoly grant in Act 118. If Field had left the implication that mere equality of treatment within legitimately defined classes of citizens was the test of conformity to the clause, Bradley laid out a number of absolute rights, identifying "certain fundamental rights which th[e] right of regulation cannot infringe," along with the guarantees in the original Constitution and the protections of the first eight amendments. He underscored how the monopoly provisions clearly exceeded the requirements of police legislation. And he concluded by examining the "mischief" that the amendment was designed to remedy. That mischief having been substantial, he argued, the amendment was broad. But if the privileges and immunities it protected were correctly interpreted, its commands would soon take on a clarity that would obviate constant federal intervention in the affairs of states.[22]

While concurring in both Field's and Bradley's dissents, Justice Noah H. Swayne nonetheless took a briefer and arguably narrower view of the Privileges or Immunities Clause in his own dissent. He explored more fully the Due Process and Equal Protection clauses with their "more simple and comprehensive terms," as he characterized them. After broadly defining life, liberty, and property, he explained that the "due process" through which they were protected "is the application of the law as it exists in the fair and regular course of administrative procedure. The 'equal protection of the laws' places all upon a footing of legal equality and gives the same protection to all for the preservation of life, liberty, and property, and the pursuit of happiness."[23]

Approaches to Interpretation

Justice Swayne's opinion leads into my second question: What interpretive approaches did the justices use? Swayne himself offered some observations on the problem of interpreting the amendment and on the judicial function. Regarding Section One, he asserted, "No searching analysis is necessary. . . . There is no room for construction. There is nothing to construe." Later, after noting that the section's terms did not restrict its protections to blacks, he protested, "This court has no authority to interpolate a limitation that is neither expressed or implied. Our duty is to execute the law, not to make it."[24]

But Justice Miller, too, claimed merely to be following the words of the amendment: "[W]e now propose to announce the judgments which we have formed in the construction of those articles, so far as we have found them necessary to the decision of the cases before us, and beyond that we have neither the inclination nor the right to go."[25]

No less a modern authority than Judge Robert Bork gives the nod for restraint, for holding to text and history, to Miller. In interpreting the amendment that "became and has remained the great engine of judicial power," says Bork, Miller displayed "caution" in "following a sound judicial instinct: to reject a construction of the new amendment that would leave the Court at large in the field of public policy without any guidelines other than the views of its members." The result was "a narrow victory for judicial moderation."[26]

Bork's assessment is plausible, for Miller's review of the Reconstruction Amendments found "one pervading purpose . . . in them all, lying at the foundation of each, and without which none of them would have been even suggested; we mean freedom of the slave race, the security and firm establishment of that freedom, and the protection of the newly made freedman and citizen from the oppressions of those who had formerly exercised unlimited dominion over him." Although only the Fifteenth explicitly "mentions the negro by speaking of his color and slavery," historical context showed each amendment "was addressed to the grievances of that race,"[27] not to claims like those advanced by the butchers. His consideration of text extended to the contextual analysis that led him to juxtapose the Citizenship Clause and the Privileges or Immunities Clause in order to narrow the scope of the latter.

Besides resorting to text and Reconstruction history, Miller used legal history, in the sense of detailing earlier documents, precedents, and authorities. Not least, he engaged in what I'll call "plain old argument," or persuasion through logical exposition. This, it needs stressing, occurred as a part of his textual and historical analyses, but its importance to his opinion warrants giving it separate mention. A clear instance is his use of a parade of horribles to refute (to his satisfaction, anyway) the idea that the Fourteenth Amendment's framers and ratifiers intended to bring under federal protection the full range of rights associated with citizenship. Were the butchers' position accepted, he warned, the Court would become a "perpetual censor upon all the legislation of the states." Other consequences would be "to fetter and degrade the state governments by subjecting them to the control of Congress" and to "radically change[] the whole theory of the relations of the state and Federal governments to each other and of both these governments to the people. . . ."[28]

Because the dissenters came to strikingly different conclusions about the protections conveyed by the Privileges or Immunities Clause, one might expect to find that they employed approaches to interpreting it that differed significantly from Miller's. But to a considerable extent they did not, for they, too, examined the text, developed the history of the Reconstruction Amendments, used legal history (documents, precedents, and authorities), and engaged in "plain old argument."

Rather than differences in kinds of approach, the question of which side went beyond text and history to read its own predilections into the Fourteenth Amendment's first section really turns on the quality of each's craftsmanship. Perhaps the most central issue is whose position on the scope of the Privileges or Immunities Clause was the more historically accurate.

To begin, it's useful to observe the way the justices "did" history in order to arrive at intent. They all reconstructed it in broad strokes and inferentially. But Field, unlike Miller, went further and consulted congressional comments. Admittedly, his probing in this regard was fairly brief, but it gives us license to ask what he and the other dissenters could have demonstrated regarding the privileges and immunities of U.S. citizenship had they pursued a more detailed inquiry into the then-recent past.

They could have turned to Senator Jacob Howard's speech introducing the amendment in the Senate on behalf of the Joint Committee on Reconstruction. In that speech, Howard reviewed the rights covered by the phrase "privileges or immunities of citizens of the United States." The related clause in the original Constitution, in Article IV, lacked authoritative interpretation from the Supreme Court, he said, so he turned to Justice Bushrod Washington's 1823 opinion in the Circuit Court case of *Corfield* v. *Coryell*. This, he told the Senate, provided "some intimation of what probably will be the [future] opinion of the judiciary" regarding the new clause.

Here, in part, is what Justice Washington had written and Howard quoted:

We feel no hesitation in confining these expressions to those privileges and immunities which are in their nature fundamental, which
belong of right to the citizens of all free Governments. . . . What
these fundamental principles are it would, perhaps, be more tedious
than difficult to enumerate. They may, however, be all comprehended under the following general heads: protection by the
Government, [and] the enjoyment of life and liberty, with the right
to acquire and possess property of every kind, and to pursue and
obtain happiness and safety, subject nevertheless to such restraints
as the Government may justly prescribe for the general good of the
whole.[29]

As examples of such privileges and immunities, Washington's list
included:

The right of a citizen of one State to pass through or to reside in
any other State, for purposes of trade, agriculture, professional
pursuits, or otherwise; to claim the benefit of the writ of *habeas
corpus;* to institute and maintain actions of any kind in the courts
of the State; to take, hold, and dispose of property, either real or
personal[;] and an exemption from higher taxes or impositions than
are paid by the other citizens of the state. . . .[30]

After quoting more of Washington's opinion, Howard continued: "To
these privileges and immunities, whatever they may be—for they are
not and cannot be fully defined in their entire extent and precise
nature—to these should be added the personal rights guaranteed and
secured by the first eight amendments of the Constitution," which
he then partly itemized.[31]

What else might the dissenters have drawn on in historically recon-
structing the intent of the clause? The modern scholarship on this
topic is a subject in itself, and I will not attempt to survey it. As an
example, however, Earl Maltz's book on the Fourteenth Amendment
is notable for its conceptually sophisticated approach to estimating the
appropriate reading of Section One.[32] From his review of the records,
Maltz recognizes that Radical Republicans described the section's
purposes in sometimes broad terms. But political reality acted as a
constraint. Republicans needed to craft and defend language that was
moderate enough to pick up the votes necessary to gain the amendment's passage.

In effect, Maltz describes Section One as meaning what it meant to its *marginal* supporters—that is, to those *least* willing to see it in broad terms. Not surprisingly, one reviewer has characterized the book as "likely to become a standard reference for today's conservatives."[33] This approach makes Maltz's conclusions all the more interesting. He finds that the Privileges or Immunities Clause embodied the bulk of Section One's protections. It constitutionalized the Civil Rights Act of 1866, thus giving protection to fundamental rights similar but not identical to those elaborated by Justice Washington in *Corfield* v. *Coryell*. It protected a set of rights that the framers found "slightly vague but not malleable." Maltz also concludes "that contemporaries must have understood the Privileges and Immunities Clause to embody most of the Bill of Rights, and they probably viewed the first eight amendments as incorporated in their entirety."[34]

Yet, when all this is said, the dissenters' very own language still makes plausible the charge that, to use our current jargon, they were "non-interpretivists" who went beyond the text of the Constitution itself and read their own preferences into it instead of restricting themselves to interpreting what it says. Field, for example, wrote that monopoly grants "are opposed to the whole theory of free government, and it requires no bill of rights to render them void." He described the Privileges or Immunities Clause as "intended to give practical effect to the declaration of 1776 of inalienable rights, rights which are the gift of the Creator; which the law does not confer, but only recognizes."[35]

But in using language like this, did the dissenters *really* break loose from text and history? It seems to me that they did not. They recurred to text, and were attempting to give it meaning. They took their guide from history—historical statements about "the rights of citizens of any free government."[36] English and American constitutional and legal history informed their arguments, as did their reconstruction of the context of the amendment's adoption. From such sources, fleshed out with what I've called "plain old argument," they found a set of rights of citizenship worthy of protection—as itemized, for example, in Justice Washington's opinion in *Corfield* and in the Civil Rights Act of 1866. True, the rights flowed from God, from nature, and from earlier arrangements of law and government; but they were protected because the text and history of the Constitution identified them and mandated their protection.

Thus, to take up a point Judge Bork raises, Field did not argue that the right to labor was constitutionally protected *because* Adam Smith had held that it was "sacred and inviolable." Rather, Field used Smith to help show the foundational quality of labor as the basis for all property, a quality that brought the right to labor within the coverage of the Privileges or Immunities Clause *if* one accepted Field's view of the new constitutional allocation.[37]

In truth, then, the dispute between the Miller and the dissenters was a *constitutional* dispute: where did the power and duty of protection lie? Not even Miller denied that a broad range of rights followed from citizenship. Quite the contrary: like the dissenters, he approvingly quoted Justice Washington's 1823 discussion of "those privileges and immunities . . . which belong of right to the citizens of all free governments. . . ." The point over which he and the dissenters differed was whether the Fourteenth Amendment now gave federal support to a broad range of rights that previously had carried only state protection.

Recent scholarship, although hardly uniform in its conclusions, suggests on balance that the dissenters had the better historically based constitutional argument. The Privileges or Immunities Clause *was* intended to protect a meaningful range of fundamental rights. It was Miller's approach of gutting this clause by reading it in light of the alleged distinction between state and United States citizenship that offended the historical record.[38]

Speculation: What Might Have Happened?

Could Field and the other dissenters have carried the day, perhaps by further exploration of the Fourteenth Amendment's actual record in Congress and before the states? In light of the five-to-four vote, the result is not inconceivable. President Grant could have provided a more tangible assist in changing the outcome if, between the first and second arguments in the case, he had appointed someone other than Ward Hunt to replace Justice Samuel Nelson. As chief judge of the New York Court of Appeals, Hunt had written an opinion upholding the New York slaughterhouse law.[39] In any event, the very closeness of the outcome encourages speculation about an "alternate world."

In their interpretive approaches, the dissenters did not depart markedly from Miller. Both sides looked to text and history—both legal history and the history of the amendment's adoption—and they refined text and history through logical exposition. As for the dissenters' apparent resort, in addition, to extra-constitutional sources, Field's and Bradley's views had a reasonably solid and detailed historical base in the framers' and ratifiers' understandings. Had the dissenters' views prevailed, in other words, the Court and other constitutional interpreters would not have received license to roam at large through unmapped constitutional territory.

Instead, if the vote had turned out five to four in *favor* of the butchers, say with the Court's opinion by Field and a concurrence by Bradley, it seems likely that a roughly mapped territory would soon have become more precisely mapped.

First, consider what we know actually did happen. The outcome in *Slaughter-House* brought interpretation of the Privileges or Immunities Clause to a halt and, in reality, largely removed it from the Constitution. As for the Due Process and Equal Protection clauses, the justices together said relatively little about them, so although a strict reading of Miller's opinion left the two clauses with narrow meanings, the issues were not argued to the point of freezing their development. In the years that followed, the doctrine we know as substantive due process slowly took shape and by the early twentieth century protected the so-called liberty of contract. But substantive due process proved too slippery to stay attached to the law of the Constitution. In recent decades, we have witnessed a revival of the doctrine (along with its equal-protection cousin) in other areas. And again the debate rages. The revived substantive doctrines are not exactly free from slipperiness.

By contrast, what might have happened if the Court in 1873 had not essentially killed off the Privileges or Immunities Clause? However much the Due Process and Equal Protection clauses eventually came to embody some of the protections covered by the Privileges or Immunities Clause when properly understood, this development took time. Had the *Slaughter-House* dissenters' views of the Privileges or Immunities Clause prevailed, its substantive protections almost surely would have become operative sooner.

Along the way, the views of Field and Bradley would have been the focus of early and sustained debate, perhaps over whose position was the correct one, to the extent that the two justices disagreed. The debate, one might imagine, would have worked itself out in the courts, among lawyers, and in public forums. It would have occurred while the origins of the clause were "fresh within the memory" of the participants, as Miller correctly noted they were in 1873, and before they became, as he said of the first twelve amendments, "historical and of another age."[40] Might such a debate have given further clarity to the clause's specific protections, protections that, even when unrefined, seem more easily comprehended than the substantive versions of due process and equal protection? And had this happened, would the Privileges or Immunities Clause, with its tangible guarantees, have proved less malleable clay in the hands of future judges than the two other clauses? Perhaps.[41]

But to return to what actually happened: the real outcome in *Slaughter-House* set the course for the development of the Fourteenth Amendment. The resulting interpretations provided a significant part of the legal environment of the *Plessy* case, decided twenty-three years later.

PLESSY V. FERGUSON

Allegedly "to promote the comfort of passengers on railway trains," Louisiana enacted a law in July 1890 "requiring all railway companies carrying passengers on their trains in th[e] State to provide equal but separate accommodations for the white and colored races." In doing so, the state became one of nine southern and border states passing separate-car laws between 1887 and 1892. Later, in 1898 and beyond, five additional states joined in. By then, in *Plessy v. Ferguson* (1896),[42] the United States Supreme Court had reviewed the Louisiana legislation and upheld the principle of equal-but-separate as consistent with the Thirteenth and Fourteenth Amendments.[43]

The first wave of separate-car laws came in the wake of new voting legislation that aimed at disenfranchising the large numbers of blacks who had continued to vote following Reconstruction and the fall of Radical governments in the South. In this regard, they were part of a broader turn to legally mandated discrimination in the middle 1880s and beyond. Another element—something of a catalyst—was interest in railway regulatory legislation, which provided an occasion for considering the separate-car laws. And not far from sight was long-existing racial antipathy, recently brought more to the foreground by charges within the white community that younger blacks who had grown up outside the confines of slavery were becoming "uppity." The formula "equal but separate" contained in the legislation had itself been used by courts for years to describe the common-law duties of common carriers toward black passengers.

The Louisiana law, which was similar to the separate-car legislation of the other states, provided that "[n]o person or persons[] shall be permitted to occupy seats in coaches other than the ones[] assigned to them on account of the race they belong to." The constitutional challenge to the law focused broadly on this provision but also involved the law's details. Besides requiring railways to provide equal facilities for each race, the legislation required conductors to make the seat assignments to the appropriate coaches or sections of coaches. Railways, conductors, and passengers not obeying the law were subject to criminal penalties, and passengers were also subject to removal from trains. Other provisions immunized companies and their officials against civil liability for ejecting recalcitrant passengers, and exempted from the law's coverage "nurses attending children of the other race."

Even before passage of the law, a group of New Orleans blacks denounced it as contrary to the basic American tenet that "all men are created equal." Appeals to principle were of no avail, however. After the votes of the state legislature's eighteen black members were no longer needed on another issue, the measure passed handily.

On September 1, 1890, blacks organized a "Citizens' Committee to Test the Constitutionality of the Separate Car Law," with members drawn largely from the city's French-speaking Creole community. One of the leaders, Louis A. Martinet, a black lawyer who was also an editor and physician, took charge of securing legal counsel. He was able to obtain without fee the services of former carpetbagger Albion W. Tourgee, by now a successful novelist and attorney in Mayville, New York, and one of the country's most prominent white crusaders for Negro rights. After some false starts, he also retained James C. Walker, a local white lawyer, who handled the Louisiana end of the test cases that emerged from the efforts of the Citizens' Committee and who eventually participated with Tourgee in preparing briefs for the U.S. Supreme Court.

On February 24, 1892, the plan laid out by the Citizens' Committee and Tourgee went into operation. Daniel F. Desdunes, the 21-year-old son of one of the committee's organizers, boarded a white car of the Louisville and Nashville Railroad with a first-class ticket for Mobile, Alabama. Although only one-eighth black—an octoroon, in the parlance of the day—Desdunes was promptly arrested, probably by prior arrangement. Once his case came before the Criminal District Court for the Parish of Orleans, Walker filed a plea challenging the court's jurisdiction on grounds that the Separate Car Law was unconstitutional. Events intervened, however. Because of delay caused partly by the mysterious disappearance of the presiding judge (an old man who apparently fell off a river levy), no ruling on the plea had come down by May 25, when the Louisiana Supreme Court handed down its decision in an unrelated case challenging the law. Because the latter court held that the Separate Car Law could not be enforced against interstate passengers, the case against Desdunes was dismissed.

Although a test of the law now awaited new arrangements, Tourgee and Walker had worked out the gist of the wide-ranging argument that they eventually took to the federal Supreme Court. Their client, they noted, was a citizen of the United States. As such, he held all the rights and privileges of citizenship, and Louisiana had no authority to condition his rights on grounds of race. In addition, section two of the Separate Car Law impermissibly clothed train officers with the authority to assign passengers on the basis of race and to refuse service. The section also made a passenger's "peaceable refusal" to comply a criminal offense. But determination of race was "a scientific and legal question of great difficulty" and could not be delegated to a train officer. In particular, the penalty of denial of passage could not rest on a train officer's summary decision as to a passenger's race, nor could criminal penalties attach to a failure to submit to his summary decision, for these provisions constituted "the imposition of punishment without [due] process of law and the denial to Citizens of the United States of the equal protection of the laws." Moreover, the rights and privileges of citizenship that were at issue pertained to passage on a public railway within Louisiana and on a common carrier of passengers between states.

The concluding point raised an interstate-commerce claim that the state supreme court's unanticipated decision had made moot. As for the argument's other constitutional "pegs," the plea on Desdunes's behalf stated: " . . . the Statute in question . . . establishes an invidious distinction between Citizens of the United States based on race which is obnoxious to the fundamental principles of national citizenship, abridges the privileges and immunities of Citizens of the United States, and the rights secured by the XIIIth and XIVth amendments to the Federal Constitution."

In early June 1892, the Citizens' Committee set up a new test case. This time the defendant was 34-year-old Homer A. Plessy, another octoroon, whose "mixture of colored blood [was] not discernible," as his counsel later described it. On June 7, he purchased a first-class ticket for Covington, Louisiana, on the East Louisiana Railway, which operated wholly within the state. Taking a seat on a coach reserved for whites, he too was promptly arrested.

Once the state filed an information against Plessy in the Criminal District Court, James Walker followed the earlier strategy of filing a plea to the court's jurisdiction. When Judge John H. Ferguson finally ruled against the plea, on November 17, Walker quickly sought review by the Louisiana Supreme Court, asking the court to take the case on writ of certiorari and to issue a writ of prohibition ordering Ferguson not to proceed. In late December 1892, the state supreme court ruled in favor of Judge Ferguson, upholding the constitutionality of the Separate Car Law. Plessy's attorneys then took the case to the U.S. Supreme Court on writ of error, where, despite the case's title, the real parties were Plessy and the state of Louisiana. Plessy's trial would await the outcome of the decision in Washington.

The Supreme Court Decides

In April 1896, nearly four years after Homer Plessy's arrest, the Supreme Court reached his case. The delay was typical in an era when the Court had far less control over its caseload than it does today. Interestingly, Plessy's lead attorney, Albion Tourgee, had hoped that time might produce a helpful change both in the Court's composition and in public opinion. But neither happened. The Court ruled against Plessy on May 18, voting seven to one to uphold the essential features of Louisiana's Separate Car Law. (One justice had missed the argument and did not take part in the decision.) The case then returned to Louisiana. In January 1897, four and a half years after his arrest, Homer Plessy formally entered a plea of guilty in Criminal District Court and was fined twenty-five dollars for violating the Separate Car Law.

The Supreme Court case produced two opinions, one for the Court by Justice Henry Billings Brown and a dissent by Justice John Marshall Harlan. The irony is obvious. Brown, a native of Massachusetts who came to the Court via Republican politics and a federal judgeship in Michigan, spoke on behalf of the white South's emerging racial settlement. Harlan, a former slaveholder from Kentucky who had campaigned against the Reconstruction Amendments after the war, spoke for a color-blind Constitution.

Harlan's dissent is often quoted, and his position on the case is better known today. Unfortunately, Brown's opinion reveals more about the constitutional climate of the late nineteenth century. (It also requires more effort at understanding, because it is atrociously composed.)

Brown quickly disposed of the Thirteenth Amendment as a basis for attacking equal-but-separate. Its inapplicability, he said, was "too clear for argument." For this conclusion he relied on the *Slaughter-House* decision and the narrow interpretation given the amendment in the *Civil Rights Cases* (1883).[44] Mere discrimination did not constitute "a badge of slavery or servitude" banned by the amendment, for, he elaborated, "[a] statute which implies merely a legal distinction between the white and colored races—a distinction which is founded in the color of the two races, and which must always exist so long as white men are distinguished from the other race by color—has no tendency to destroy the legal equality of the two races, or re-establish a state of involuntary servitude."[45]

With that, Brown turned to the Fourteenth Amendment. In *Slaughter-House,* Brown noted, the Court had held that the amendment only prohibited "hostile legislation of the states [abridging] the privileges or immunities of citizens of the United States, as distinguished from those of the states." But the Court had not "offered any expression of opinion as to the exact rights [the Fourteenth Amendment] was intended to secure to the colored race."[46] As a result, Brown had to ask what those rights were—or, more precisely, whether the Louisiana law infringed rights protected by the amendment.

Brown addressed several specific objections to the Louisiana law that Plessy's counsel had argued. They had claimed, for example, that the law violated the right of equal protection by immunizing railway officials against civil suits arising from its enforcement, thus depriving passengers of a right of action that was available to other persons. Brown noted that the state itself conceded this section was unconstitutional. Counsel also had argued that because of its mechanism for assigning seats, the law could, without due process, deprive Homer Plessy of the valuable property that was represented by his reputation as a white. Brown responded that a white person who was improperly assigned to a colored coach could seek damages, while a black person assigned to a colored coach had no right to a reputation as a white.[47]

Plessy's broad and fundamental objection, however, was that the Separate Car Law violated the ban on racial distinctions embodied in the Citizenship and Privileges or Immunities clauses of Section One. Brown saw the central issue differently, contending that *Plessy* "reduce[d] itself to the question whether the statute of Louisiana is a reasonable regulation. . . ." Translated, this meant that the amendment's prohibitions did not extend to regulations that were "reasonable," but Section One does not mention reasonableness. Brown took the concept instead from previous cases interpreting police regulations and the amendment. From them, he drew the rule that "every exercise of the police power must be reasonable and extend only to such laws as are enacted in good faith for the promotion of the public good, and not for the annoyance or oppression of a particular class."[48]

The problem then became how judges could test for "good faith." In this regard, Brown's reasonableness test proved lax, to say the least. After he asserted that the question reduced itself to whether the Separate Car Law was reasonable, he added:

> . . . with respect to this there must necessarily be a large discretion on the part of the legislature. In determining the question of reasonableness it is at liberty to act with reference to the established usages, customs, and traditions of the people, and with a view to the promotion of their comfort, and the preservation of the public peace and good order. Gauged by this standard, we cannot say that a law which authorizes or even requires the separation of the races is unreasonable, or more obnoxious to the Fourteenth Amendment

than the acts of Congress requiring separate schools for colored children in the District of Columbia, the constitutionality of which does not seem to have been questioned, or the corresponding acts of state legislatures.[49]

By this point in his opinion, moreover, he had already laid the groundwork for an expansive view of "reasonableness" in the area of race regulations. He did so partly by observing that "laws permitting, and even requiring, . . . [separation of the races], in places where they are liable to be brought into contact, do not necessarily imply the inferiority of either race to the other, and have been generally, if not universally, recognized as within the competency of the state legislatures in the exercise of their police power."[50]

But Plessy's core argument constituted a claim that the amendment made race distinctions unreasonable as a matter of law—period. Not so, replied Brown. His language is a little curious to the modern reader:

The object of the amendment was undoubtedly to enforce the absolute equality of the two races before the law, but, *in the nature of things,* it could not have been intended to abolish distinctions based upon color, or to enforce social, as distinguished from political, equality, or a commingling of the races upon terms unsatisfactory to either.[51]

Why was this true "in the nature of things"? The answer lay in the limitations of "legislation" (a term which Brown here used broadly to include constitutional amendments):

Legislation is powerless to eradicate racial instincts or to abolish distinctions based upon physical differences, and the attempt to do so can only result in accentuating the difficulties of the present situation. If the civil and political rights of both races be equal one cannot be inferior to the other civilly or politically. If the one race be inferior to the other socially, the Constitution of the United States cannot put them upon the same plane.[52]

Brown's premise is only thinly veiled: race instincts exist and are rooted in man's nature to the point that law cannot eradicate them.

The doctrine of equal-but-separate was thus consistent with the

Fourteenth Amendment. The amendment's framers and ratifiers surely did not intend it to ban reasonable regulations reflecting truths inherent in the nature of things. Nor did legally mandated separation itself "stamp[] the colored race with a badge of inferiority." The conclusion of inequality resulted "solely because the colored race chooses to put that construction upon it."[53]

Justice Harlan Dissents

John Marshall Harlan disagreed across the board. As his central proposition, he held that an equality of rights flowed from United States citizenship. "In respect of civil rights, common to all citizens," he wrote, "the constitution of the United States does not, I think, permit any public authority to know the race of those entitled to be protected in the enjoyment of such rights."[54] The source of this right was the Thirteenth Amendment's outlawing of badges of servitude and the Fourteenth's protection of the rights of citizenship. "These notable additions to the fundamental law were welcomed by the friends of liberty throughout the world," he asserted. "They removed the race line from our governmental systems."[55] Quoting from an earlier case, he explained that while " 'the words of the [Fourteenth] amendment . . . are prohibitory, . . . they contain a necessary implication of a positive immunity or right, most valuable to the colored race,—the right to exemption from legislation against them as colored; exemption from legal discriminations, implying inferiority in civil society. . . . ' "[56]

For Harlan the Separate Car Law's requirement of racial separation was enough to establish its unconstitutionality. He recognized, however, that Louisiana and Justice Brown had an answer: the law was motivated, not by a desire to discriminate on the basis of race, but by the need to promote the health, welfare, and morals of the public. It was a reasonable police measure that bore equally on citizens of both races; and because it was reasonable, it met the test of the Fourteenth Amendment. This was nonsense, argued Harlan, in an appeal to common sense:

Every one knows that the statute . . . had its origin in the purpose, not so much to exclude white persons from railroad cars occupied by blacks, as to exclude colored people from railroad cars occupied by or assigned to white persons. . . . The thing to accomplish was, under the guise of giving equal accommodation for whites and blacks, to compel the latter to keep to themselves while traveling in railroad passenger coaches. No one would be so wanting in candor as to assert the contrary.[57]

In addition, Harlan argued that if states could condition access to public transportation on racial distinctions, they could pass a host of similar laws, and even restrict mixing on grounds of religion. But, ran the state's and Justice Brown's answer, such extensions of legislated separation would be held *un*reasonable. So Harlan examined the concept of reasonableness itself. His discussion on the point unfortunately lacks clarity, but he seems to have meant that in assessing constitutionality, courts properly have no business examining the *extent* to which a measure promotes policy goals. Legislation either falls within a legislature's proper sphere, or it does not. If it does not, its policy advantages will not save it.[58]

This brought Harlan to his often-quoted language: "Our constitution is color-blind, and neither knows nor tolerates classes among citizens. In respect of civil rights, all citizens are equal before the law."[59] The cases pertaining to reasonableness cited by Louisiana (and, by implication, those cited by Justice Brown) had no bearing on the Louisiana act. They came, he said, from times and places marked by racial prejudice. They could not "be guides in an era introduced by the recent amendments to the supreme law, which established universal freedom to all born or naturalized in the United States, and residing here, obliterated the race line from our systems of governments, national and state, and placed our free institutions upon the broad and sure foundation of the equality of all men before the law."[60]

Finally, Harlan turned to another constitutional provision. The system of state-mandated discrimination legitimated by the Court's decision violated Article IV's guarantee to every state of a republican form of government. As a consequence, offending state legislation could be attacked through congressional legislation, or by the courts as part of their duty to uphold the supreme law of the land.[61]

Approaches to Interpretation

The concern for text and the history of the Reconstruction Amendments that had informed the opinions in the *Slaughter-House Cases*
reemerges in the *Plessy* opinions, although in an attenuated fashion. The
resort to legal history and to "plain old argument" appears as well. But
whereas in *Slaughter-House* none of the opinion-writers significantly
moved beyond the Constitution and its history—not even the dissenters, who had at least intimated a warrant *in* history for turning to
fundamental law—the justices in *Plessy* went further. Justice Brown
clearly turned to a new source for enlightenment. Justice Harlan did so
too, although in a subtle fashion that arguably took him back to history,
to the origins of the Constitution, and again beyond the Constitution.

It is instructive to observe the constitutional text at issue in the
portion of Brown's opinion that addressed the Fourteenth Amendment. Today, we tend to think of *Plessy* as an equal-protection case.
Actually, the only equal-protection issue that Brown isolated was
Plessy's claim that the railroad-immunity provision of the Separate
Car Law denied him a cause of action (a suit for civil damages) that
was open to others. To the extent that Brown based a conclusion on
a specific clause of the Fourteenth Amendment's first section, it was
the Due Process Clause. This occurred when he briefly (and dismis-
sively) addressed Plessy's claim that the Separate Car Law deprived
him of property in the form of his reputation as a white person.[62]

Brown's main focus instead was on Section One as a whole. He
was obliged to deny that the rights claimed by Plessy flowed from
any provision within Section One. In doing so, he did not analyze
its language but rather turned to legal history. "The proper construction of this amendment," he wrote, "was first called to the
attention of this court in the Slaughter-House Cases. . . ." But
because they "did not call for any expression of opinion as to the
exact rights it was intended to secure to the colored race," he had
to look further.[63]

In looking further, Brown turned to the amendment's "original"
history only inferentially. Because law simply could not accomplish
certain objectives (like changing social attitudes), he inferred that the
amendment's originators could not have intended to attain them. His

understanding of the amendment derived mainly from other sources: the legal history of race-related regulations and legislation, the post-ratification history of the Fourteenth Amendment outside the area of race, and popular and scientific thought about race.

From state, lower federal, and a few Supreme Court cases involving race distinctions, Brown extracted evidence that separation by race under the principle of equal-but-separate was *reasonable*. Although they displayed some variation, the cases typically involved common-law suits by blacks against common carriers for unlawful ejection from coaches or other facilities. In these actions, by the 1880s and early 1890s judges most often ruled that separation promoted the public welfare and thus fell within a carrier's authority, so long as equal facilities were provided to passengers of each race paying the same fare.

Justice Brown also confronted the issue of reasonableness as a general requirement under the Fourteenth Amendment. Here the Court's non-racial decisions came to bear. We commonly have the image, I think, of late-nineteenth-century courts using the amendment to strike down state police measures regulating perceived social ills and economic relationships. In actuality, most challenged measures passed judicial scrutiny. A person held his liberty and property on the condition that they were subject to reasonable regulations, said the judges; and classifications, too, were permissible so long as they were reasonable.

Because the reasonableness doctrine required at least an arguable relationship between a challenged police measure and the health, welfare, or morals of the public, it took Brown into the area of racial thought. To some extent the accumulation of lower-court decisions, along with the non-judicial pronouncements embodied in the related regulations, evidenced a substantial body of opinion that racial separation served a public purpose. But Brown additionally had an extra-legal source to drawn on.

Recall Brown's claim that "in the nature of things" the amendment "could not have been intended to abolish distinctions based upon color. . . ."[64] Later he asserted that law "is powerless to eradicate racial instincts, or to abolish distinctions based upon physical differences."[65] He did not provide citations for these assertions, but he easily could have. They found their warrant in contemporary scientific views of race and in comparable popular views. It is likely, in fact, that Brown was well versed in the relevant literature. He had been a member of the American Social Science Association and followed current intellectual developments. Evidence suggests, too, that he thought the law should take account of current scientific knowledge, for two years after *Plessy* he explained that law is "to a certain extent a progressive science."[66]

What passed for good science and social science in the late nineteenth century included positions that today appear blatantly racist. Respectable studies depicted races as fitting along a hierarchy, with differing *inbred* intellectual endowments, proclivities for criminal behavior, and tendencies toward diseases. Race gave rise to instincts, one of which was aversion to members of other races. Nonetheless, race mixing posed a major threat, for hybridization would pull down the European race. The beginning of wisdom was to recognize that separation made scientific sense. In 1895, for instance, anthropologist Daniel G. Brinton explored the status of the various races in his presidential address to the prestigious American Association for the Advancement of Science. For him, the idea of "a racial mind, or temperament of a people" was as demonstrable as distinctive physical traits. He concluded that the differences between mankind's "component social parts, its races, nations, tribes . . . , supply the only sure foundations for legislation; not *a priori* notions of the rights of man. . . ."[67]

Racial thought such as this allowed Brown to speak confidently of "the nature of things," and his reliance on it marks the significant difference between his opinion and the opinions in *Slaughter-House.* True, he gave less attention than did Justice Miller and his colleagues to probing the text of the amendment and the history of its adoption, yet he at least took bows toward those sources. His reliance on legal history (documents, precedents, and authorities) ran in a largely different direction from that charted in *Slaughter-House,* for the amendment had now been operative for over two decades; but the opinion-writers in 1873 had by no means neglected legal history itself. (They looked to earlier periods, however.) Brown's opinion also used "plain old argument," though it plays somewhat less of a role than it did in the *Slaughter-House* opinions. What was absent in *Slaughter-House* is reliance on science as a key to man's nature. In *Plessy,* science provided Brown an essential (albeit tacit) link in proving reasonableness, as well as the basis for inferring the Fourteenth Amendment's restricted intent.

Constantly stressing the rights of "citizens," Harlan reached a conclusion vastly different from Brown's. In one respect, however, his interpretive approach was similar to Brown's, for he refrained from associating rarefied doctrines with any of the specific clauses of Section One of the Fourteenth Amendment. While his argument related especially to the Citizenship and Privileges or Immunities clauses, he at least implicitly kept the whole first section in view, along with the Thirteenth Amendment. For him, the two amendments taken together, "if enforced according to their true intent and meaning, [would] protect all the civil rights that pertain to freedom and citizenship."[68]

In giving meaning to Section One as a whole, Harlan relied partly on the history of its formation and adoption. He spoke of "the beneficent purposes which the people of the United States had in view when they adopted the recent amendments," and mentioned in this regard the granting of citizenship to blacks and the protection of the privileges and immunities of both state and U.S. citizens.[69] But he eschewed any detailed examination of the times and relied instead on past Court decisions for specifics. In the process, he drew broader conclusions from them than they warrant on careful reading, and he neglected the obviously narrowing result in *Pace* v. *Alabama* (1883), where the Court had upheld an anti-miscegenation law.[70] Basically, he took the rights flowing from citizenship as a given; his focus on them was unadorned by close analysis of text, history, or case law.

Harlan instead aimed his detailed argument at examining the implications of the majority's conclusions. Among other things, this task took him into his three parades of horribles, depicting the kinds of racial assorting to which Brown's position could lead, the juror segregation it would justify, and the further racial strife it would produce.[71] Overall, he thoroughly battered Brown with "plain old argument."

In the end, as we saw earlier, Harlan abandoned the Reconstruction Amendments altogether and linked his position to the Guarantee Clause, the Constitution's guarantee to the states of a republican form of government. The *Plessy* principle, he contended, left the states with a power, "by sinister legislation, . . . to place in a condition of legal inferiority a large body of American citizens, now constituting a part of the political community, called the 'People of the United States,' for whom, and by whom through representatives, our government is administered." Such a system violated the Republican Guarantee Clause and thus fell within the authority of Congress and the jurisdiction of the judiciary to dismantle.[72]

Although Harlan tied his position here to a constitutional provision, he pushed beyond the text in giving meaning to "republican government." For him, the concept meant more than institutional forms. It required treating citizens as individuals without respect to race. The idea of republican government, that is, is inconsistent with majority decisions contrary to the principle that all men are created equal.[73]

Yet this understanding is not significantly different from Harlan's core position on the Thirteenth and Fourteenth Amendments; and the skimpiness of his textual and historical analysis of the amendments suggests that he also went beyond text and history in finding their meaning. To be sure, he may only have decided that his long dissent thirteen years earlier in the *Civil Rights Cases,* where he had provided an extended and detailed analysis of the amendments, made it unnecessary to provide another full examination. Still, it seems significant that as he turned from examining the force of the amendments to his Guarantee Clause argument, he pronounced the Separate Car Law "hostile to both the *spirit* and letter of the constitution."[74]

What was the spirit he thus evoked? Why did both the Republican Guarantee Clause and the Reconstruction Amendments embody its commands? Harlan surely had read Albion Tourgee's brief. In it, Tourgee had relied partly on the Declaration of Independence, which, he explained,

> is not a fable as some of our modern theorists would have us believe, but the all-embracing formula of personal rights on which our government is based and toward which it is tending with a power that neither legislation nor judicial construction can prevent. . . . It has become the controlling genius of the American people and as such must always be taken into account in construing any expression of the sovereign will. . . . This instrument not only asserts that "All men are created equal and endowed with certain inalienable rights, among which are life, liberty, and the pursuit of happiness," but it also declares that the one great purpose for which governments are instituted among men is to "secure these rights."[75]

If Harlan meant to follow Tourgee and go beyond the Constitution in this fashion, he thereby turned to the document that Abraham Lincoln saw as the "apple of gold" for which "the *Union,* and the *Constitution,* are the *picture* of *silver.*"[76] In their *Slaughter-House* dissents, of course, Justices Field and Bradley had turned to the same document, but they had rooted the principles of the Declaration more identifiably *within* the history of the founding of the republic. At the very least, Harlan's departure from text and history to "the broad and sure foundation of the equality of all men before the law" contrasts fundamentally with that of Justice Brown, who founded his argument on the understanding of man's nature proffered by contemporary science.

Speculation: What Might Have Happened?

The close vote in *Slaughter-House* makes it at least plausible to think the decision could have gone the other way. By contrast, the lopsided vote in *Plessy* means that, in all likelihood, nothing within the power of Plessy's attorneys or Justice Harlan could have reversed the outcome. Still, to plumb the case's importance, it is useful to ask "what if . . . ?"

What if the Court had endorsed Harlan's reading of the Fourteenth Amendment as it pertained to race? The clearest result would have been the invalidation of separate-car laws throughout the South. Whether other than state-mandated discriminatory practices would have fallen seems more problematic. It is conceivable, I suspect, that despite the rights Harlan saw as attaching to citizenship *per se* (or flowing from the Republican Guarantee Clause), judges would have narrowed the sweep of the ruling so as to allow the continued existence not only of social discrimination but also of segregation by quasi-public entities. The common law of common carriers had allowed racial separation pursuant to company rules well before states had mandated it. If, however, the Court had proceeded beyond a Harlanesque outcome in *Plessy* and had soon reversed itself on the issue of the *Civil Rights Cases,* then congressional legislation aimed at directly protecting civil rights rather than merely remedying state violations *might* have made a difference. Over the long run, anyway, we perhaps would have been spared the pretextual use of the Commerce Clause as a grounding for equal rights.

Perhaps, too, adopting Harlan's interpretive approach in *Plessy* might have nudged the Court back toward broadly resurrecting the protections of the Privileges or Immunities Clause from their *Slaughter-House* grave. Certainly the justices would have had the opportunity to do so as they grappled with the widening range of economic and social regulations and questions of criminal process arising by the late 1890s. Pursuing this hypothetical outcome requires a still greater stretch of the imagination, not to mention more suspension of incredulity. (Harlan himself often went in the opposite direction, taking a permissive stance toward police legislation.[77]) But to play the game: one possibility is that the Court would have taken its guidance by turning at large to the realm of political philosophy, directly plumbing the meaning of the Declaration of Independence and the content of natural law and right. More likely, however, as lawyers in an age of increasing professionalization, the justices would have eschewed such reaches. After all, "pre-moderns" though they were, even Justices Field and Bradley had not founded their *Slaughter-House* conclusions on the Declaration alone; they turned to history and text, to Blackstone's *Commentaries* and Justice Washington's *Corfield* opinion, and to a variety of other cases, to determine the specific content of the privileges or immunities of citizenship.

Nonetheless, broadly resurrecting the Privileges or Immunities Clause would almost surely have tightened the emerging Fourteenth Amendment tests for "reasonableness," with significant implications for judicial review of economic and social regulations. This carries us back to my speculations on *Slaughter-House*. It seems unquestionable that the privileges or immunities of citizenship were better defined in prior law and history than were the emerging substantive restrictions associated with the Due Process and Equal Protection clauses. Being less slippery, they might not have tightened to the point of triggering the reaction that occurred against substantive due process in the late 1930s and beyond. As a result, might we today see greater uniformity in the degree of scrutiny to which differing kinds of governmental regulations are subjected? Perhaps. But just as easily—if not more likely—twentieth-century intellectual trends and common-law approaches to judging would long since have worked their effect, washing out alternative outcomes in either *Slaughter-House* or *Plessy*.

These speculations and questions are perhaps as vain and idle as

Justice Miller's interpretation made the Privileges or Immunities Clause. They call to mind one further question, however. Will modern historical scholarship on the Fourteenth Amendment ever affect modern judicial interpretation to the extent of calling judges committed to text and history consistently and rigorously back to text and history?

3

On the Structure of Privacy: *Adair* and *Coppage* Revisited

HADLEY ARKES

According to legend, the relation of the New Deal to the courts turned one day in 1937, during the litigation over the National Labor Relations Board and the power of the federal government to compel the recognition of unions. In a cluster of three cases, the Supreme Court sustained the Roosevelt administration and the new regime of unions. Justice George Sutherland joined the dissenters in all three, but he was moved to write an opinion only in *Associated Press* v. *National Labor Relations Board*.[1] There, Sutherland thought that the policy of the federal government, in promoting unions, was treading on the freedom of the press affirmed in the First Amendment.

In the course of his opinion, Sutherland offered this analogy: Let us suppose that there were a statute with the same objective as the statute under review, but that the law sought its end by forbidding the discharge of employees who had *refused* to join a "labor association."

Let us suppose further that a labor association is engaged in publishing an interstate-circulated journal devoted to furthering the interests of labor, and that members of its editorial staff, resigning

---

Hadley Arkes is the Edward Ney Professor of Jurisprudence and American Institutions at Amherst College. Among the books he has written is *Beyond the Constitution* (1992).

45

their membership in the association, transfer their allegiance from the cause of the working man to that of the employer. Can it be doubted that an order requiring the reinstatement of an editorial writer who had been discharged under these circumstances would abridge the freedom of the press guaranteed by the First Amendment?[2]

I am tempted to say that Sutherland's argument was clinching, but which case did it clinch? I am not persuaded that Sutherland found here an arrangement that distinctly threatened the freedom of the press. But I do think he touched something at the core of a necessary freedom of association in private settings. We might put the question this way: Would the problem be different in any morally significant respect if we removed the feature of a journal or a newspaper? What if we had instead a lobbying group organized to promote "abortion rights"? What if it turned out that key members of the staff had suffered a jolt to their convictions and persuaded themselves finally that abortions were unjustified in most cases? And what if they were determined, nevertheless, to keep their jobs? Would the organization be so narrow-minded as to fire these competent people because of their moral and political views?

In the way that principles are casually bandied about these days, a firing of this kind will often bring the charge, by earnest commentators, that the case presents a problem under the First Amendment. In this woolly construction, the First Amendment is engaged whenever someone suffers a cost, or even a telling reproach, on account of views he has expressed. But of course, the First Amendment was meant as a restraint *on the government.* The danger apprehended was the prospect of acting through the force of law to restrain publication, or to inhibit the expression of political arguments through the threat of legal punishment. The First Amendment is not threatened when voters withdraw support from candidates who take stands they find uncongenial. Nor was it threatened when a producer refused to hire Vanessa Redgrave on account of her public attacks on Israel.

The life of a republic begins with the freedom of people to press their interests in a public politics. In that respect, there is an evident connection between the right to engage in the public discourse and the right to associate for political ends. A group constituted for the purpose of advocating an expansive right to abortion would have a presumptive right to confine its association to people who shared its ends. To remove an opponent from the payroll could not be a violation of the First Amendment. And to remove a dissident from the staff of a newspaper could not be a violation of his right to publish. After all, he is not legally barred from publishing. He must merely suffer the strains of finding himself another job, and another outlet for his writing.

But with an apt symmetry, it could be said, with the same reasoning, that the right engaged on the side of his employer is not the right to publish. That right, more generically, is the right to associate for legitimate ends. That right of association need not be narrowed or confined to political ends. The example of groups directed to political ends has the advantage merely of bringing out more dramatically the nature of the right engaged in the case. That right was in fact engaged in these cases on the National Labor Relations Board, because it was bound up with the policy of overriding the claims of private association in the name of imposing unions on private employers. Sutherland's conviction about the wrongness in the case of the Associated Press was finally rooted in his conviction about the wrongness of compulsory unions. And in the course of his argument he said: "The right to belong to a labor union is entitled to the shield of the law, but no more so than the right not to belong. Neither can be proscribed. So much must be true, or we do not live in a free land."[3]

Sutherland drew here on the pristine clarity of the classic cases on unions, whose decisions had been grounded in the understanding of natural rights. Those decisions, in *Adair* v. *United States* (1908) and *Coppage* v. *Kansas* (1915), had begun with the premises of personal freedom, with the notion that the worker, or the person, was the owner of himself, with the prime authority to commit his own labor.

A Modern Misinterpretation

This brief dip into the case of the Associated Press has the advantage of reminding us that the politics of a republic depends on the freedom of groups and persons to press their interests in public; and that freedom must depend, in turn, on a structure of privacy, or a line that marks off, unambiguously, a domain of private association. Of course, no group may claim the right to draw the curtain of privacy over a criminal conspiracy. It may not use privacy as a shelter for wrongdoing. But if people have a right to press their legitimate interests in politics, they must have an ancillary right to preserve the integrity of their interests by confining their associations to the persons who truly share their commitments and their ends. That means that a decision to fire people under these circumstances, to deprive them of their jobs or sustaining contracts, cannot be taken as a violation of their freedom of speech or their right to preserve their own political convictions. For we could honor such a claim on their part only by denying to other people the very same claim to sustain an organization committed to their own, legitimate ends.

But the point seems to have escaped some people on the current political scene: the First Amendment cannot be violated by private organizations, in withdrawing contracts or firing people from their jobs. The freedom of speech can be impaired, in a manner relevant to the Constitution, only when a government works *through the instruments of the law* to restrain speech or to punish its utterance. And by that standard it should be clear that there is no violation of the First Amendment when the government acts, not by imposing legal penalties but by withholding grants.

Much has been said in recent years, in an outbreak of hyperbole, about the "gag rules," the federal regulations that forbid the promotion or counseling of abortion in clinics that receive federal funds. The campaign of opposition to these regulations can become intelligible only on the premise that the withholding of a grant is the equivalent of a legal penalty. And yet, no one working in a clinic has been threatened with the prospect of a fine or injunction for speaking about abortion. A clinic and its counselors remain free to counsel or even incite people to abortion; but they may not be sustained by federal money as they engage in that project. If these people insist that the withholding of a grant must be regarded as the equivalent of a legal penalty, they undermine the domain of privacy that must be a critical support to the very scheme of a republican politics. For under those premises, we could install the situation that Sutherland described in his hypothetical case: a union newspaper could be compelled to preserve on its staff an editor who was out of sympathy with its cause; and an organization committed to a "right to abortion" may be compelled to retain in its ranks employees who were determined to resist this project.

To hold, then, that the withdrawal of a grant is equivalent to a legal penalty is to take a position that must be at odds with any arrangement that preserves a domain of privacy and a population of private citizens who are enfranchised to engage in politics. The irony is that there is no faction in our politics right now more adamant than the "pro-choice" party in insisting that the withholding of grants amounts to a legal penalty and a violation of the First Amendment. But that is to say, no group is more at odds right now with the premises of privacy than the group that has made the protection of privacy the sovereign premise and the reigning slogan in its jurisprudence.

And yet, that discrepancy should no longer come as a surprise. For two decades now, the people who have professed the deepest concern about "privacy" have also been those most determined to extend the controls of the federal government to all varieties of private associations in order to ban discriminations based on race and gender. First, the law reached private inns, restaurants, and theaters, but then private businesses of all sizes, even those with only the most tenuous connection to interstate commerce. In the last few years, these regulations have been extended, under the laws of the states, to cover even private clubs.

In the case of abortion, a "private choice" has been treated as a "public good," which deserves to be supported by public funds and promoted at every turn. Until the passage of the Civil Rights Restoration Act of 1988, the party of abortion sought to use the controls of the civil-rights laws for the sake of compelling private universities to recognize abortion as a right, to perform the surgery in their hospitals, and to include abortion in their medical plans. In sum, the party of abortion has shown a marked unwillingness to permit the rest of us to withdraw into the private enclaves of our reticence or opposition.

The partisans of abortion might have been restrained in this movement if they had truly cultivated, over the years, a respect for the premises of privacy. Those premises are clearly revealed in the classic cases at the beginning of this century dealing with the question of unions. If we returned to those cases, we would find a compelling argument made for a structure of privacy, a structure that cannot depend, for its boundaries, on refined shades of reasoning. But that statement for privacy at its deepest level would also cast up certain barriers to the partisans of abortion, as they would try to use the levers of the government for the sake of annexing to their cause the funds and the commitment of private businesses, private colleges, private persons.

ADAIR V. UNITED STATES

The early cases on unions have by now been assigned to the dark, reactionary past of the Supreme Court. They are charged to the record of those whimsical jurists who managed to persuade themselves that there really were such things as "natural rights," and that those rights could encompass the freedom of any person to make his living at a common trade. The decision of the Court in *Adair* v. *United States*[4] offers a crisp expression of natural rights, and that sense of the case should be confirmed by the recollection that this decision was written by the first Justice John Marshall Harlan. The man who wrote that moving dissent in *Plessy* v. *Ferguson* ("[I]n the eye of the law, there is in this country no superior . . . class of citizens. . . . Our Constitution is color-blind") could hardly be put down as a reactionary. The jurist who thought that the Thirteenth Amendment could be used to reach private conduct and strike at the lingering incidents and badges of slavery was hardly a man who could be charged with a crimped understanding of rights.

In fact, it helps us to grasp the meaning of *Adair* if we recognize that the decision reflected the understanding of those judges who had come through the Civil War, remade the American regime, and established the citizenship of black people. One judge in this period remarked, in a passage quoted often, that it was "preposterous" that unions should replace slaveholders and "attempt to issue orders that free men are bound to obey."[5] That is to say, the decision in *Adair* is understood in its proper frame when we understand that Harlan and his colleagues began with the same premises that established the wrong of slavery. They began with the claim of any human being, or moral agent, to his own, natural liberty, and to the ownership of himself.

The *Adair* case arose under a federal statute, an act of 1898 that sought to protect a freedom for workers, in interstate carriers, to preserve membership in unions.[6] The act made it a crime to fire workers for the offense of joining a union. The federal government claimed to reach, with these regulations, only firms engaged in operations among the states, and it purported to act here for the sake of regulating interstate commerce.

Mr. Adair's Discriminatory Act

William Adair was an agent, in Kentucky, and a master mechanic in charge of hiring, for the Louisville and Nashville Railroad. The railroad extended its operations from Kentucky into Tennessee and Ohio, and so the company came within the coverage of the federal act. In October 1906, Adair discharged O. B. Coppage, a member of the Order of Locomotive Firemen, from his employment with the railroad. Coppage brought a charge under the federal law that Adair did "unjustly discriminate against him" because of his membership in a labor union. Adair pleaded not guilty, but he was convicted under a section of the law that provided a fine for any employer

> who shall require any employee, or any person seeking employment, as a condition of such employment, to enter into an agreement, either written or verbal, not to become or remain a member of any labor corporation, association, or organization; or shall threaten any employee with loss of employment, or shall unjustly discriminate against any employee because of his membership in such a labor corporation, association, or organization. . . .[7]

If these restrictions were reasonable or defensible, then they could have been seen as a plausible part of the power of Congress to regulate interstate commerce. But Harlan and his colleagues did not regard these measures, finally, as defensible, and they rendered their conclusion through the formula contained in the Fifth Amendment: namely, that the statute restricted Adair, in his liberty and property, without due process of law. Of course, the bill had been passed in a formally correct way, and it bore all the formal attributes of a law. To say then that Adair was restricted in his liberty and property "without due process of law" was to say that he was restricted unreasonably, without justification. Harlan said that Adair had suffered an "invasion of . . . personal liberty, as well as of the right of property."[8] The accent was placed on personal liberty, because the right of property found its ground in the premises of personal liberty. John Locke had taken this matter to the root in the "Second Treatise on Government": The ownership of property begins with the ownership of ourselves. We have a claim to the fruits of our own labor, or the work produced with our own hands, only if we ourselves are the owners of our own hands. We would not be the owners of our hands if we were slaves and our hands belonged to someone else. The right to exercise that sovereign authority in the commitment of our own labor, or the making of contracts about our own labor, is the first right of property.[9]

The Symmetry in Natural Freedom

The judges who had come out of the Republican movement had begun, in their jurisprudence, with this premise of natural freedom: that human beings are by nature the owners of themselves, and they are the owners of their own labor. Only they can determine the conditions, or the terms, on which that labor is committed to others, *or withdrawn.* And so Justice Harlan would establish, as one of his anchoring points in the *Adair* case, that it could not be within the authority or functions of government, "at least in the absence of contract between the parties . . . to compel any person, against his will, to perform personal services for another." Every person has a natural right "to sell his labor upon such terms as he deems proper," and a right "to quit the service of the employer for whatever reason."[10] That decision to quit the service of an employer does not have to be justified unless the employee is breaking a contract. If the decision to quit a job had to be justified, we would be installing the premise that the labor of a man belonged, presumptively, to the employer or to the state. For why else would he have to justify to an employer, or to a court, the exercise of his personal freedom? Anyone who takes seriously the premise of natural freedom would certainly have to say, with Harlan, that the worker is free to quit his job at any time "for whatever reason."

But in that case, as Harlan recognized, there has to be a symmetry between the freedom of the worker and the freedom of the employer. For clearly, the employer is no less of a natural man than the employee. He has no less of a claim to his own natural freedom, and therefore, his freedom of association can hardly be less than that of his employee. As Justice Harlan remarked, "The right of a person to sell his labor upon such terms as he deems proper is, in its essence, the same as the right of the purchaser of labor to prescribe the conditions upon which he will accept such labor from the person offering to sell it."[11] The freedom to join a union, or any other legitimate association, was simply implicit in the standing of any free man. But that freedom cannot entail the power to compel another man, against his will, to join the same association. For that kind of compulsion is clearly at odds with the freedom of the other man to determine *his* own associations. And for the same reason, the employer has to be equally free: he has to be no less free to enter into an association with workers who are members of unions or to refuse that association, for any reasons *he* regards as sufficient. The employer must be free to consider whether he should preserve his association with a man who holds membership in, say, a union, a church, or the Ku Klux Klan. That decision, on his personal associations, is implicit in *his* natural freedom. The employer might well decide, in the same way, to promote a union, and to hire only the members of a union. And that, too, would come within his proper freedom, even though it would put a certain pressure on workers to join that union.

As Harlan pointed out, Coppage had retained the freedom to quit his association with the railroad at any time he chose, no matter how unwise that decision might be. And Adair had to retain a comparable freedom to quit his association with Coppage, no matter how unwise *that* decision might be. Harlan was utterly certain, then, that "the employer and the employee have [an] equality of right, and any legislation that disturbs that equality is an arbitrary interference with the liberty of contract which no government can legally justify in a free land."[12]

That symmetry had to be in place unless there was something in the circumstances of the railroad, or interstate commerce, that justified a tipping of the balance and the adding of restrictions to one side rather than the other. But it was evident that the work on the railroad could be performed even by men who were not members of the unions. Therefore, there was no need to require, or encourage, membership in unions for the sake of carrying on interstate commerce. And if there was no need to require unions, it was even less warranted to assign, in effect, to unions a power to bar people from jobs solely because they were not members of the union. As Harlan observed, there was simply no logical or necessary connection between the work of the railroad and membership in a union.[13] The federal statute had seriously restricted the personal freedom of Adair, and the rights of property of an employer, for reasons that bore no necessary connection, then, to the end of regulating interstate commerce.

Enshrining "the Flow of Commerce"

As the last ploy of a weak argument, there was a descent into the facile, low claim that unions would help preserve interstate commerce from the dangers of disruption—that is, the disruption caused by the strikes and violence produced by unions. Years later, during the New Deal, the same argument surfaced, and Justice James C. McReynolds met it in a joltingly direct way: If the harm to be averted was the harm produced by a strike, why not act directly to forbid the strikes and the violence? Why go about matters in such a roundabout way, and commit the further offense of accepting such a shabby moral argument? The Congress had postulated the interruption of interstate commerce as a harm that justified the exertion of federal authority, while abstracting entirely from the moral question of whether the interruption was caused by conflicts that were justified or unjustified. If the decisive point was to preserve the stream of commerce, then, as McReynolds asked, could it "become the duty of the Federal Government hereafter to suppress every strike which by possibility may cause a blockade in that stream?"[14] In that same vein, McReynolds raised these further questions:

> May a mill owner be prohibited from closing his factory or discontinuing his business because to do so would stop the flow of products to and from his plant in interstate commerce? May employees in a factory be restrained from quitting work in a body because this will close the factory and thereby stop the flow of commerce? . . . If the business cannot continue with the existing wage scale, may Congress command a reduction?[15]

Could any of these conditions have extended the reach of the federal government merely because they might interrupt the flow of commerce? By the time McReynolds was writing in dissent, the Court was on the threshold of accepting such an unconfined reach of the Commerce Clause. McReynolds had to expend his outrage in a dissenting opinion, but in the *Adair* case, Justice Harlan could write for the majority in taking notice of the sleaze in the argument and decorously turning aside from it. Harlan remarked, with some delicacy, that the judges would not impute to the Congress a purpose of according to members of a union privileges that are withheld from another class of workers serving the same employer. And he would not make the defamatory assumption that members of unions will "resort to illegal methods for accomplishing any particular object they have in view."[16]

Freedom of Contract, Despite Disparities

The liberal wags would later remark that the "liberty to contract" protected the right of the worker to contract for over sixty hours of work per week at less than a legislated minimum wage. The symmetry of rights between employers and workers was held to be cynical fiction. As the argument ran, there could be no real freedom of contract while there were grave disparities in the bargaining position of the employers and the employees. And so Justice Oliver Wendell Holmes remarked, in his dissenting opinion in *Coppage* v. *Kansas* seven years later, that

> a workman not unnaturally may believe that only by belonging to a union can he secure a contract that shall be fair to him. . . . If that belief, whether right or wrong, may be held by a reasonable man, it seems to me that it may be enforced by law in order to establish the equality of position between the parties in which liberty of contract begins.[17]

Of course, a worker may plausibly believe that his bargaining position in relation to his employer could be enhanced if he were connected to the Mafia or the Ku Klux Klan. But nothing in that estimate should make any difference to the question whether an employer, or any other person, has a right to refuse an association with a member of the Mafia or the Ku Klux Klan. And yet, this cliché of legal realism has been repeated so persistently by the historians that one would hardly know that the judges addressed the question—and answered it conclusively. It would be hard to find a more precise address to that challenge than the opinion written by Justice Mahlon Pitney for the Court in *Coppage* v. *Kansas,* the case that followed directly on the precedent established by *Adair.*

Justice Pitney was sufficiently clear-headed to recognize that virtually all contracts may take place on conditions of disparity between the parties. Each party is seeking to gain something in the possession of the other; each is hoping to attain some advantage and improve his position. There is a sudden turn in the market in real estate, and we find a buyer's market, with many people, previously thought to be quite secure, finding themselves pressed to turn their assets into cash. When the market turns back, may the former sellers sue to regain the added price that their houses could fetch in a seller's market? Could they argue that there was something unfair or wrong about the contract they made because they had been at a serious disadvantage?

Pitney took matters to the root: If we have a free economy, with rights of property, "there must and will be inequalities of fortune." And "unless all things are held in common," it was "self-evident," as he said, that "some persons must have more property than others."[18] Therefore, it should also be evident that, in most cases, a contract will not involve two parties with a perfect, or even a near, parity of wealth. And so, Pitney remarked, "each party when contracting is inevitably more or less influenced by the question whether he has much property, or little, or none." In "the nature of things," it is "impossible to uphold freedom of contract and the right of private property without at the same time recognizing as legitimate those inequalities of fortune that are the necessary result of the exercise of those rights."[19] Every day contracts important to both parties are made by parties that are not the least equal. A worker in a factory may contract to buy a car, with monthly payments, from a dealer representing General Motors. It may be in the interests of both parties to make that contract. There are vast disparities between them, but both sides are thought to have the competence to weigh their interests and make a commitment that will be regarded as enforceable.

A contract implies parties competent to contract, but the test of competence cannot be wealth. What the workers involved in these cases had to have was the competence of "free agents" or mature adults. If those workmen had been subjected to coercion or intimidation, Justice Pitney had no doubts that the government could seek to bar that coercion as a means of protecting people and insuring the integrity of contracts.[20] The judges had already upheld legislation that sought to protect workers from fraud and manipulation in the payment of wages *(Knoxville Iron* v. *Harbison)*. Justice Rufus W. Peckham, in *Lochner* v. *New York,* had approved those restraints on the freedom of contract, and beyond that he had observed that "[t]he State . . . has the power to prevent the individual from making certain kinds of contracts . . . [e.g.,] a contract to let one's property for immoral purposes, or to do any other unlawful act."[21] The judges could never be called on, justly, to enforce a contract for prostitution, or a contract to carry out a murder. Peckham acknowledged, in that same opinion, that the state may limit the freedom of contract for the sake of protecting the health and safety of workers, as for example in smelting plants *(Holden* v. *Hardy)*.

In all these ways, the law could establish layers of moral conditions as the limiting grounds for a contract. The question remaining, then, was whether the law could properly refine those moral conditions even further by barring employers from refusing to associate with unions and their members. And that issue would turn on whether there was something in principle wrong in the decision of a private person to turn away from others because of their membership in unions.

COPPAGE V. KANSAS

That question was at the heart of the case in *Adair,* and the same question in principle was presented in *Coppage* v. *Kansas,* even though the case involved a state rather than a federal statute, and even though the ground of the case had to be shifted from the Fifth Amendment to the Fourteenth. A statute in Kansas in 1903 made it unlawful for employers to require, as a condition of employment, that an employee detach himself from a union, or pledge not to become a member of a union. In the case at hand, Coppage was a superintendent of the St. Louis and San Francisco Railway Company. He had presented to a switchman named Hedges an agreement for his signature. In that contract, Hedges would have to agree to withdraw his membership in the Switchmen's Union of North America as a condition for continuing with the company. But Hedges refused. Justice Pitney and his colleagues were clear that the *Adair* decision should be controlling because the issue was in point of principle the same.[22] The Court would of course shift from the Due Process Clause of the Fifth Amendment to the Due Process Clause of the Fourteenth Amendment, but the same arguments in principle that proved decisive in the *Adair* case had to be quite as decisive in *Coppage*.

For the sake of sharpening and confining the central question, Justice Pitney was willing to remind his readers of the many limitations the Court was willing to uphold on the freedom of contract. As those limitations confined more precisely the domain of contract and private choice, the question was whether the law was intruding into a domain of private judgment, which would have to be left entirely to the governance of the person himself. The Court was convinced that it was now dealing with a rudimentary freedom of association that could not be accommodated, coherently, with the kinds of statutes involved in *Adair* and *Coppage*. And for the sake of illuminating that central point again, Justice Pitney was willing to elaborate even further on the argument offered by Justice Harlan in the *Adair* case.

On the right of any workman to join a union—or a church, or a ball club, or any other legitimate association—the judges never suffered a tremor of doubt. And it was also implicit in the same freedom that the worker had a right to quit his job if his employer refused to hire people who were not members of his union. If that right could be held by individuals, it could be held by aggregates of individuals: all members of a union had the freedom to walk off a job *en bloc* if they recoiled from the prospect of working alongside people who were not members of their union. If workers had a right to join a union, and to take this action in concert, then they certainly had the right to confine their association to people who shared their commitment. "Can it be doubted," asked Pitney, "that a labor organization—a voluntary association of working men—has the inherent and constitutional right to deny membership to any man who will not agree that during such membership he will not accept or retain employment in company with non-union men?"[23] The freedom of association entailed the right to restrict, or confine, membership in that association.

But then, taking the matter from the other side, the right of a workman to join a union could *not* entail a "right to join the union without the consent of that organization" and its members.[24] The workman's freedom of association could not trump, or override, the right of the other workmen to preserve their own association on their own terms, for that would contravene *their* freedom of association. But then, conversely, it had to follow that the union could not demand that an unwilling person be assigned to the union. If a worker had no inclination to join a union, the union had no moral ground on which to compel his membership. Nor did it have any moral ground on which to claim the further right to deny a man access to a job unless he joined a union he had no wish to join. Hence the curious inversion that took place: The right of a workman to join a union was rooted in the premise of his natural freedom to commit his own labor; but then the unions were claiming the power to prevent a free man from committing his labor to a legitimate job with a contract he was willing to make. And that is why a judge could write that passage mentioned earlier, in *In re Higgins*, that it was "preposterous" that unions should replace slaveholders and "attempt to issue orders that free men are bound to obey."

There had to be a symmetry in the freedom to join an association and the freedom to refuse to join it, for they both sprang from the same principle. But for the same reason Justice Pitney was compelled to point out again that the employer could have no less a claim to his own freedom of association. If the members of a union had to be free to refuse their association to persons they found uncongenial, the employer surely had the same freedom to shun an association with members of unions. Pitney asked, "Can there be one rule of liberty for the labor organization and its members, and a different and more restrictive rule for employers?"

> We think not; and since the relation of employer and employee is a voluntary relation, as clearly as is that between the members of a labor organization, the employer has the same inherent right to prescribe the terms upon which he will consent to the relationship, and to have them fairly understood and expressed in advance.[25]

All these deductions could be made, fairly, from the logic of the "freedom of association," for they involved simply a rejection of those claims that were self-contradictory, claims that could not cohere with a primary right, on the part of a free agent, to engage in legitimate associations. And from this chain of argument Pitney could draw the further conclusion that "the liberty of making contracts does not include a liberty to procure employment from an unwilling employer."[26] That, too, seems to emerge from the same unbreakable chain of deductions. And yet it would seem to contradict the premises contained in the Civil Rights Act of 1964, along with all of the succeeding acts that have sought to restrict the freedom of private businessmen to make their own, private judgments as to the clients they will serve and the employees they will hire.

In fact, there has been a new willingness to look again at the Civil Rights Act and raise questions that run to the root of that law.[27] The arguments made by the Court in *Adair* and *Coppage* would supply, I think, the most piercing arguments to challenge the Civil Rights Act at its foundation. Or to put it another way, an apt test for the Civil Rights Act is whether it could be defended against the postulates that Harlan and Pitney put so carefully into place, as they marked off a hard perimeter of private association and personal freedom.

Anyone trying to build the case for the Civil Rights Act might be tempted to look first to the dissenting opinions in *Adair* and *Coppage*. There, I must say, he would find little help, but with an ironical turn, he might do better in looking to Justice Harlan—not the opinion written for the majority in *Adair* v. *United States,* but the notable dissenting opinion over twenty years earlier in the *Civil Rights Cases.*[28] For in those landmark cases, Harlan defended a law on public accommodations that could reach, with federal authority, and prescribe the terms of association in private inns and restaurants. Harlan himself may contain the ingredients for solving the puzzle.

Justice Day Dissents

But before I reach Harlan, I would like to follow some threads that may be cast up by the dissenting opinion in the Coppage case. I fear I would try the patience of my readers if I sought to conduct them through the terrain covered by the fog of Mr. Justice Day's dissent in *Coppage*. Among the odd equations and analogies contained in that argument, there is a strange willingness to treat on the same plane a legal restriction and a private discrimination. As I suggested earlier, there would be a critical difference between a refusal to hire Vanessa Redgrave out of an aversion to her political views, and a scheme of restraint in which she is blocked by law from appearing on the stage or expressing her views. The latter case may represent a violation of the First Amendment; the former could not.

Justice Day was willing to regard the freedom of association as a fundamental, constitutional right. In his reckoning, the refusal of an employer to associate with a union represented a violation of that right, as much as any legal regulation that forbade people to form unions. And so, Day could argue—in a manner that deeply misconceived the case—that the statute sought to protect "the exercise of a legal right, by preventing an employer from depriving the employee of it as a condition of obtaining employment."[29] But nothing done by the St. Louis and San Francisco Railway could deprive Hedges of his freedom to join a union. He retained that freedom even if he were barred employment at the railroad; and in fact, he was barred from the railroad only because he quite emphatically manifested his freedom, by refusing the terms offered to him.

It could hardly have been said that Hedges bore an "unalienable" right to join a union, a right that he could not have been expected to waive as part of a contract for employment. For under that logic, Hedges could not alienate that right himself; he could not himself refuse to join a union. But not even the defenders of unions were willing to argue that membership in unions was a logically necessary good, which overrode the freedom of the worker to make his own judgments about the associations that merited his commitment.

Day leaped then to rather different ground and argued that the employer could not require, as terms of employment, "terms that are against public policy."[30] Apparently, it was the public policy of the state to promote and protect unions. That was, of course, a massive begging of the question, which had to remain: How could the state be justified in establishing a public policy that abridged the axiomatic claim of a free agent to the most rudimentary freedom of association? In the course of the argument, Day cast up a suggestive possibility, a hypothetical that is worth pondering:

[A]n employer may be of the opinion that membership of his employees in the National Guard, by enlistment in the militia of the State, may be detrimental to his business. Can it be successfully contended that the State may not, in the public interest, prohibit an agreement to forego such enlistment as against public policy?[31]

But with this example Day recast the problem: he began with a defensible commitment of public policy that had nothing to do with private employers. Let us make the example even stronger and assume that the political community created an obligation for the citizen to military service. Then the question might be, If a legislature created an obligation to military service, could it protect the people who bore that obligation? Could it protect them against the loss of jobs at the hands of private employers who would fire them for no reason other than the fact that they were meeting their legal obligation?

But even when the problem is cast in these terms, the answer is not unequivocal. Not all businesses can afford to function with key jobs going unattended, and not all businesses can practicably guarantee that the job will be there when the man returns from military service. For these and many other reasons, Congress has been cautious in legislating in this field. From what I recall, Congress has been disposed to deal with the problem by offering incentives and rewards rather than forbidding employers, outright, to replace men who are meeting their obligations in the service. But that is to say, there are serious considerations of equity, serious questions of principle, that would caution against laying down a uniform rule in this way for private businesses of all sizes and descriptions.

Yet there is a more modest application of this argument that I rather regret has not been tried. During the 1970s there was a move on college campuses to force the disclosure of contracts between members of the faculty and the Central Intelligence Agency. The purpose of that move was to expose both the associations that might have existed in the past and the contracts for research that might have been in place at the time. The claim was made that these relations, held in confidence, were inconsistent with the nature of an academic place. But that argument, I am sure, could be shown to be untenable. The real political purpose was to discredit the CIA, and to drive off the campuses the members of the faculty who were willing to collaborate with their government. It seems a shame that the Administration did not take advantage of the premises established for the protection of unions and seek to protect these people on the campuses. If the government has a legitimate interest in conducting certain operations for the national security, and cloaking them in secrecy, then the government would have a legitimate interest in protecting those operations from public disclosure. The Congress might have legislated simply to protect these people and operations from disclosure at the hands of private institutions. And yet, as far as I am aware, the government did not take the slightest step in this direction, to impose even that modest restraint on private colleges and universities.

Day's line of argument inspires, however, another hypothetical. Let us suppose that it was the "public policy" of a state to practice capital punishment. The execution of prisoners would not, of course, offer full-time employment, so let us suppose that the executioner works most of the time as a custodian in a Catholic college. Let us assume that the administrators of the college bear strong objections to capital punishment, grounded in religious convictions, and they do not wish to be associated with a man who makes capital punishment a minor business. They request that he give up his moonlighting in operating a gas chamber as a condition for remaining at the college. If he is unwilling to give up this sideline, they suggest that he spare the college the embarrassment of this association. I find it hard to imagine that the state would claim a ground for legislating here to protect the executioner from the adverse judgment of a private college. The college would clearly be refusing to honor a practice that has been incorporated as part of the "public policy" of the state, and yet I doubt that the state would claim a right to intervene in that private association for the sake of revising that adverse judgment.

In all the hypotheticals I have cited here, the government could begin with a policy that flows out of a plausible commitment of the laws. And yet, in all these instances, as I have suggested, we would find a deep reluctance to protect those commitments of the law by crossing the boundary that separates the public and the private, and laying down rules for private associations. But this reluctance to invade the domain of privacy should have been even deeper when it came to protecting unions or establishing the conditions of employment. For the government would not begin there with any commitment that arises from the central functions of the government itself. A government will need to manage a national defense and create obligations for military service; but it will have no compelling need to promote unions.

Still, it might seek to promote unions for the same reason that it would seek to protect the health and safety of workers, or ban discrimination based on race. The government may be animated by the passion to do justice, and it may believe (wrongly, in my judgment) that the policy on promoting unions has the same moral grounding as the propositions that enjoin us not to draw any judgments about the character and worthiness of people on the basis merely of their race.

Stepping Over the Public/Private Line

Since the Civil Rights Act of 1964, there has been a new willingness to cross the barrier between the public and the private, and to lay down the most copious, intricate rules for ordering the relations between private businessmen and their clients and employees. For years, the federal government had been reluctant to cross that barrier, even after the extensions of the Commerce Clause under the New Deal. The only lingering ground of reservation was the understanding reflected in those earlier cases of *Adair* and *Coppage:* namely, that there must still be a domain of private action, in which a person remains free to enter an association or quit it, to marry or decide at the last moment to back out, to take on a partner or turn away from him for reasons she would not be obliged to justify to anyone else. And that is what it had to mean, at some rudimentary level, to be a free agent with a claim of natural liberty, to be the owner of oneself.

The Supreme Court affirmed that understanding in 1883 when it rejected the Civil Rights Act on public accommodations. The judgment of the Court pivoted on the need to recognize a necessary line that separated the public from the private. Justice Harlan himself accepted that distinction, as he would years later in the *Plessy* case and in the cases dealing with unions. Even in dissent, in the *Civil Rights Cases,* he wrote:

> I agree that government has nothing to do with social, as distinguished from technically legal, rights of individuals. No government ever has brought, or ever can bring, its people into social

intercourse against their wishes. . . . I agree that if one citizen chooses not to hold social intercourse with another, he is not and cannot be made amenable to the law for his conduct in that regard; for even upon grounds of race, no legal right of a citizen is violated by the refusal of others to maintain merely social relations with him.[32]

Private discriminations might be unwarranted, but they were protected by the shelter of privacy, and they were still notably different from a policy that proclaims the inferiority of black people as a public doctrine and enforces the segregation of black people through public law. The state may not impose policies of segregation—but then Harlan made a turn: neither may those policies be imposed by "any corporation or individual wielding power under State authority for the public benefit or the public convenience."[33] Here, Harlan made a distinction between what he called "a mere private boarding house" and an inn, which may be subject to the regulations of a common innkeeper.[34] Places of public accommodation—inns, restaurants, even places of amusement—were "established and maintained under direct license of the law. The authority to establish and maintain them comes from the public."[35] And in turn, the authority to license begat the authority to prescribe rules.

But here, Harlan certainly presumed too much, and presumed too casually. He was altogether too willing to follow Chief Justice Morrison Waite in *Munn* v. *Illinois* in identifying businesses "clothed" with a public interest.[36] And he was altogether too willing to pass over Justice Stephen Field's warning that a business does not become a public agency merely because a large portion of the public has an interest in it. As Field remarked, "A tailor's or a shoemaker's shop would still retain its private character, even though the assembled wisdom of the State should declare . . . that such a place was a public workshop, and that the workmen were public tailors or public shoemakers."[37]

Years later, in *Plessy* v. *Ferguson*, Harlan would insist that a railroad was the equivalent of a public highway, subject to the regulations of public law. But *Adair* and *Coppage* both involved railroads. If we followed the line described by Harlan in marking off the public and the private, we might have to conclude that the employers in *Adair* and *Coppage* could not claim the standing of private persons to establish the terms of their own private associations. And yet, it is conceivable that Harlan could have held to his judgment against unions even while holding to his settled conviction that railroads were the equivalent of public utilities. For one part of his argument in the *Civil Rights Cases* was that nothing in the federal act impaired the private nature of these private businesses, even though the government would prescribe the terms on which they would admit blacks to their establishments.

Harlan in the *Adair* case and Harlan in the *Civil Rights Cases* seemed to teach two different lessons about privacy and the reach of the law. To reconcile these two opinions by Harlan would require a rather refined argument, which would begin at this point: In Harlan's construction, the law on race and public accommodations did not intend to displace private owners with a public management, following the directions of a public authority. The law left private businessmen free to direct their operations in all aspects that were distinct to their business. As Harlan put it, "[The law] does not assume to define the general conditions and limitations under which inns, public conveyances, and places of public amusement may be conducted, but only declares that such conditions and limitations, whatever they may be, shall not be applied so as to work a discrimination solely because of race, color, or previous condition of servitude."[38]

Harlan touched here on an ancient understanding. Let me recall some of the expressions that may be more familiar to us. Plato raised the question of whether a man with self-control was weaker than a man who knew no restraint, and whether a polity subject to the restraint of a constitution was weaker than a polity in which power was unconstrained. The man with self-control was stronger, and the polity governed by the restraints of lawfulness was a stronger polity. No one had a "right to do a wrong," and a polity restrained from wrongful acts, or from acts it had no right to undertake, was not restrained from any power it had a right to exercise. Rather, it was free to flex its powers and its genius in considering that wide universe of things it could rightfully pursue.

In the same way, it could be argued that a law that restrained an inn from discriminating on the basis of race did not impair anything in its character as an inn. The inn remained free to take in clients and offer meals, and the vexing details that had to be arranged in managing that business would still be in the hands of its private owners. The privacy of the business was left intact; the owners were merely restrained from doing things that were wrong, and wrongful things could not be a necessary part of any legitimate business. With a similar understanding, Harlan had argued in *Adair* that Congress had the authority to regulate interstate commerce, but that the Constitution could not give Congress a license to impose a wrongful rule in the name of regulating commerce. And when the Court struck down this wrongful regulation, it in no way diminished the power of Congress, for Congress remained free to regulate the full breadth of commerce that it could rightfully reach.

Now, of course, when Congress passed the Civil Rights Act of 1875, it affected quite noticeably the freedom of private businessmen to decide on the terms of their own associations. They were barred from refusing an association with black customers, as employers were barred, in the act of 1898, from refusing an association with members of unions. Clearly, the difference between the two cases could not turn, for Harlan, on whether the business was in private hands. The difference had to turn on an understanding of why it was truly wrong in principle to turn away from customers on the basis of race, and why it could not be wrong in the same way for a private owner to refuse an association with members of unions.

Harlan sought to argue forcefully that Congress was justified in imposing the restraints on racial discrimination, and he argued even more luminously in showing that Congress could not have been justified in imposing unions on private owners. I have sought to show in another place that Harlan was not fully clear about the ground of his argument in principle about discriminations based on race.[39] But my own judgment is that his sense of the matter overall would prove correct. If we could take the space here to trace the matter back to its moral axioms, I think we could make an interesting case: the same propositions that establish the claim of a moral agent to his personal freedom would establish the wrong of judging a man by his race, or compelling a man to accept a relation to a union.

That, however, would require a rather exacting, strenuous argument, calling upon the discipline of the moral philosopher. I think it is a sound argument, but it requires a larger exertion of philosophic competence than most judges, recently, have been able to summon. Harlan's colleagues seemed to be guided by Burke's dictum that "refined policy is ever the parent of confusion." Their inclination seemed to be to avoid a jurisprudence that was overly refined. They preferred to draw the line between the private and the public more sharply, and accept the shortfalls from a more exacting justice. They were willing to give a wide latitude to legislatures to restrict private business for the sake of protecting the health and safety of workers and customers. They were even willing to accommodate restrictions of the more familiar, traditional "vices." But they were powerfully reluctant to tread on a delicate system of personal relations when it came to working out the connections between people of different races in private settings, or fixing the moral terms of personal relations, whether they involved the rules of a club, the recognition of unions, or the setting of wages.

The judges tried to write here, as I said, with a large, uncomplicated hand. The line they drew would not satisfy a more demanding sense of justice, and indeed Congress reached some notably different judgments about the commands of justice and the allowances of the Constitution. But what might be said on behalf of the judges is that the line they drew was prudent and intelligible, and its prudence stands out more strongly when viewed against the experience of our own day. During the past three decades, the Civil Rights Act of 1964 has been at the center of the dramatic changes that have come about in relations between the races in this country. No one who knows the good done by that act would readily will its undoing. But anyone who has seen the massive corruptions brought about through the laws bearing on discrimination in employment, anyone who has seen the new waves of regulations and the expanding volume of litigation, will know the corruptions that can be wrought even by the impulse to do justice.

In principle, the scheme of justice contained in the Civil Rights Act of 1964 was quite defensible. But we have had a political class of judges and legislators who have not been able to modulate their teachings and manage this scheme of justice. In the light of our experience, we might judge ourselves to have been better off with a policy that observed clearer boundaries between the public and the private. The jurisprudence of the earlier judges might have given us a law that was prudent and defensible, even though it could not supply a more exacting justice.

A Subtle View of Privacy

But still, where does that leave the question of "privacy"? What of that zone in which people are free to reach judgments without the need to render a justification to anyone else? We have lingered over the differences between Harlan and his colleagues, but if we put their opinions together again, we would find that the judges in that period left the question of privacy in a far more subtle and complicated state than anything struck off by the wit of our current judges.

For one thing, those earlier judges did not name a zone of privacy that may furnish a complete shelter from the law. They did not think that anything in the domain of private choice established a "right to do a wrong" so long as it was carried out behind private walls. They understood, to the contrary, that the claims of freedom could be made only by an agent with moral competence, who had the faculty for directing his freedom to moral ends. There were moral grounds for the claims of private association, and the law could impart a structure that limited, even further, the kinds of decisions that could be made, rightfully, in that zone of private action. Contracts could not be made for immoral ends. The right of ownership over oneself could not be used as a ground for inflicting injuries on others, or even on oneself.

The difference between the public and the private was a critical distinction that could not be allowed to disappear in its refinements. A private discrimination was different from a discrimination imposed with the force of law. A private turning away was different from a legal restraint, enforced with a penalty. But the line that marked the division between the private household and the public street could not mark a moral distinction, and it could not always bear a jural weight. A private murder is just as wrong as a murder in a public street, and the law may reach that private murder even if it takes place in the sanctuary of the bedroom.[40] If an abortion can be shown to be an unjustified homicide, then it cannot be part of any "right of privacy." But at the same time, if people claim that we cannot pronounce on the rightness or wrongness of abortion, if that decision must be left to private choice and private judgment, then there is no ground for imposing the choice of abortion through the levers of federal law. There would be no warrant for invading private associations and compelling private colleges and private corporations to fund abortions in their medical plans. And if we find ourselves with a national plan of health insurance, there will be no justification for excluding from the program doctors and hospitals that refuse to perform abortions.

The judges understood in the past that there was no principle that could establish the necessary rightness of joining unions. Therefore, there was no ground on which to displace the authority of private employers in making their own private judgments. And in the same way, if we cannot show that any wrong is done in turning away from abortions, then we cannot be justified, in any larger degree, in compelling private corporations to support abortions. Where we cannot speak with moral authority, there the law should preserve a decorous silence. And what is left is that domain in which a person is free to reach any judgment he would, without the need to render a justification to anyone else.

The structure of privacy, then, would not be bounded by any non-moral attribute like the wall of a house; nor would it be marked by formal rules that are empty of moral significance. Harlan and his colleagues seemed to understand that the domain of privacy was the domain of the innocent, the legitimate, and the morally indifferent. They knew that the law could penetrate and limit that domain, and whether it did or not would depend finally on the moral substance of the case. It would depend on the layers of reasoning and evidence supplied by the legislators, as well as the judges, as they sought to explain the differences they found in these cases—as they sought to explain just how they would know that it was deeply wrong to turn a man away from an inn on account of his color, or why it would not be wrong for a worker, or an employer, to turn away from a union. We explain all that we need to explain when we recall the paths of reasoning that led a judge like George Sutherland to his conclusions, and permitted him to say, with a settled confidence, that "so much must be true, or we do not live in a free land."

4

Constitutional Rights in a Federal System: Rethinking Incorporation and Reverse Incorporation

AKHIL REED AMAR

At the founding of our country, rights were limited by federalism: the federal Constitution guaranteed one set of rights against state governments, and a different set against the federal government. For example, the "takings" clause of the Fifth Amendment applied to the federal government and not the states, whereas the "contracts" clause of Article I, Section 10, applied to the states and not the federal government. This ordering was reflected in the landmark 1833 Supreme Court case *Barron* v. *Baltimore*, which held that the entire Bill of Rights, as originally designed, applied only to the federal government and not to the states.

Today, in light of post-founding developments—most importantly, the reconstruction of the nation that occurred after the Civil War, when the Thirteenth and Fourteenth Amendments were added—the question is: Do federalism limits largely drop out when we think about

Akhil Reed Amar is Southmayd Professor of Law at Yale Law School. He is the author of many articles on the Constitution and is currently working on a book about the Bill of Rights.

rights? For example, does the Bill of Rights now generally apply to the states in a way that at the founding it applied only to the federal government? In particular, should freedom of speech and of the press, which in the First Amendment are applied against the federal government, now apply against the states? If so, why?

These questions are closely tied to the so-called incorporation debate: Was the Fourteenth Amendment designed to "incorporate" various provisions of the Bill of Rights against the states? And the flip side is the so-called reverse-incorporation debate: Should equal-protection principles, which are specified in the Fourteenth Amendment in connection with the states, apply against the federal government as well? We will look first at the incorporation debate in a 1907 case, *Patterson* v. *Colorado,* and then turn to the reverse-incorporation debate in a 1954 case, *Bolling* v. *Sharpe.* The two debates present some interesting symmetries.

INCORPORATION IN THE PATTERSON CASE

At issue in *Patterson* v. *Colorado* was whether the principles of free speech and free press applied against the states.[1] A Colorado newspaper had printed articles and a cartoon criticizing and mocking the state supreme court justices. As a result, the Colorado Supreme Court held the publisher of the newspaper in contempt, even though the Colorado legislature had never passed any law authorizing judges to punish non-litigants who happened to speak out against a court and its decisions. There was no jury trial in *Patterson,* for in those days contempt of court could be tried without a jury, even though cases as early as *Zenger* (1735) had dramatized the special importance of jury trials in free-speech and free-press matters.[2]

The question the U.S. Supreme Court confronted in *Patterson* was: Do the justices in Colorado have the authority to throw a person in jail or fine him because he criticized a decision they had reached? And the Court, through Justice Oliver Wendell Holmes, said that the Colorado justices *could* do this—it was constitutional and did not offend the Fourteenth Amendment. Justice Holmes was willing to concede, for the sake of argument, that First Amendment principles of free speech and free press applied against the states. But, he claimed, these principles were limited to a prohibition against prior restraint. No prior restraint had occurred in *Patterson,* and therefore the state justices could do whatever they wanted.

Here is Holmes's language:

> We leave undecided the question whether there is to be found in the Fourteenth Amendment a prohibition similar to that in the First. But even if we were to assume that freedom of speech and freedom of the press were protected from abridgment on the part not only of the United States but also of the States, still we should be far from the conclusion that the plaintiff in error would have us reach.[3]

So, even "assuming" for the sake of argument that the First Amendment applied to the states via the Fourteenth, the Court nevertheless upheld the action in question. That is basically the same move that the Court would later make in *Gitlow* v. *New York,*[4] assuming for the sake of argument something that later became the established doctrine of the Supreme Court—"incorporation" of the First Amendment against states—without, frankly, a lot of elaboration or justification.

The central question that both *Gitlow* and *Patterson* present is: Why *should* states be limited by these freedoms of speech and press even though the First Amendment says that "*Congress . . .* shall make no law . . ."? I believe that a strong case can be made for the incorporation of most of the provisions of the Bill of Rights against the states, and that it is easiest to make with regard to the freedom of speech and of the press. Let me offer some reasons for that intuition, and for the belief that what the state justices did in *Patterson* was outrageous and unconstitutional.[5]

Structural and Textual Arguments

First, the argument for incorporation is what might be called a *structural* argument, a global interpretation of our constitutional system. Our system is a democracy. It is built on the idea of popular sovereignty, the idea that persons in government are agents of the electorate—they are servants, not masters. In order for this popular sovereignty to work, voters must have great freedom to criticize, even mock, those in power. If government officials could immunize themselves against criticism, the people would not be sovereign—the government would. And structurally, it should make little difference whether government suppression of citizen criticism takes the technical form of prior restraint or of after-the-fact punishment; either way, the effect is to chill citizen speech critical of incumbent officials.[6] This is not just a moral argument or an argument from justice; it is an argument about the foundation of our constitutional system.

But is there a textual basis for it? Good structural arguments can often be teased out of particular patches of text. Let's look at the first three words of the preamble to the Constitution, "We the people," and the concluding words, "do ordain and establish this Constitution. . . ." Here is a dramatic textual embodiment of the American theory of popular sovereignty, the idea that the people created the government and that government officials are accountable to the people. These words, of course, are not limited to the federal government or the states but are preambulatory to the entire Constitution and therefore the entire system of American constitutional government.[7] And under the Supremacy Clause of Article VI ("This Constitution, and the laws of the United States which shall be made in pursuance thereof . . . , shall be the supreme law of the land . . ."), the idea of popular sovereignty is as applicable to states as to the federal government.

Another patch of text is even more directly on point: the Republican Government Clause (sometimes called the Guarantee Clause). Article IV says that each state must have a republican form of government. Therefore the state of Colorado cannot transform itself into a monarchy, or a system where government is sovereign. A republican form of government is one in which the people ultimately rule, through law—through state constitutions, through a federal constitution.[8] In the nineteenth century, several leading lawyers were willing to point to the Republican Government Clause as the foundation for the idea that political speech, speech about government officials and the propriety of their actions and policies, was obviously constitutionally protected.[9]

Let me make this point one other way, and again this is a structural argument of sorts. If the speech in question is really about a national issue—something like slavery in the antebellum era—how can any state try to shut down this national speech within its jurisdiction? Isn't that fundamentally the same kind of constitutional violation that Chief Justice John Marshall identified in *McCulloch v. Maryland* (1819), where a state was trying to shut down a national bank? If a state cannot be allowed to shut down a national bank, why should it be allowed to shut down a national debate?[10] And if the speech in question is about a local or state rather than national issue, the Republican Government Clause deprives state government of the right to invade the sovereignty of the citizenry on this matter. The citizens must be able to deliberate and to criticize those in government.

Now let's move to the First Amendment, which says that "Congress shall make no law . . . abridging the freedom of speech, or of the press. . . ." Since it specifies *Congress,* perhaps, one might argue, this amendment leaves the states free to violate the freedoms of speech and press.

There are several problems with that argument. To begin with, even if there were no First Amendment, the general theory of popular sovereignty and a theory of enumerated federal power (i.e., that the federal government has only the powers specifically given to it in the Constitution) actually would have imposed great limits on the ability of Congress to restrict political speech. In that sense the First Amendment, like the Tenth Amendment, is simply a declaration and affirmation of the preexisting constitutional system. There is a real problem, however, in reading that affirmation as, in effect, a negation of other rights that might be retained by the people, including rights against states. The Ninth Amendment, although it may not be a source of independent rights, at the very least counsels great hesitation before we deduce that because the First Amendment says Congress *cannot,* that necessarily means states *can,* abridge the freedom of speech and of the press: "The enumeration in the Constitution, of certain rights, shall not be construed to deny or disparage others retained by the people."

Nor does the mere fact that the First Amendment says *Congress* mean that the *President* is free to impose a censorship edict, or that *federal courts* are free to put people in jail for expressing their political opinions. In the famous 1971 Pentagon Papers case, for example, the *President* was trying to censor the press; but no one said that First Amendment principles of free speech and a free press therefore did not apply.

This is a point made by the first Justice John Marshall Harlan in his dissent in *Patterson:* "No one, I take it, will hesitate to say that a judgment of a *federal court,* prior to the adoption of the Fourteenth Amendment, impairing or abridging freedom of speech, or of the press, would have been in violation of the rights of 'citizens of the United States' as guaranteed by the First Amendment."[11] Harlan says, in effect, that we must read the First Amendment at a different level of generality from what that word *Congress* implies. Clearly federal courts cannot put people in jail for expressing political opinions. Why not? In part, because of the theory of popular sovereignty, and in part, because of the theory of separation of powers. If even Congress cannot authorize federal courts to punish or censor speech, surely federal courts should not be able to do so on their own. So again we see how certain structural ideas, like popular sovereignty and separation of powers, fit into our articulation of rights.

At the founding, the First Amendment phrasing "Congress shall make no law" was meant in part as a federalism device, saying there was simply no enumerated power over speech, press, religion, and the like. The language of the First Amendment was an inversion of the language of Article I, Section 8, the Necessary and Proper Clause: "The *Congress shall* have power . . . to *make* all *laws* which shall be necessary and proper . . ." (emphasis added). Thus, the power to restrict speech is not given to the federal government. To try to use commerce power, taxing power, or other enumerated power to punish or censor speech would be a pretextual use of those powers that would offend the spirit of enumeration.

The Declaratory Argument and Reconstruction

None of this is to say, however, that states are not also similarly constrained. The theory of popular sovereignty applies to them as well as to the federal government. They too are constrained by the idea that there are rights that the people "retain," to use the phrasing in the Ninth Amendment. The First Amendment speaks of *the* freedom of speech and of the press as if this right were a preexisting entity. If it is preexisting, then why would states be any more free than the federal government to violate this right? I will call this theory—which was very prominent in the antebellum era, especially among Abolitionists—the declaratory theory.[12] The idea is that although the First Amendment has a federalism component—affirming the Article I, Section 8, idea that there is no federal enumerated power over speech, press, religion, and the like—the amendment also does more than that: it declares that there is such a thing as *the* freedom of speech and of the press, and that this declaration should be taken seriously, even in regard to state power.

State judges, in trying to think about limits on state power, might look to the federal Constitution for law-finding guidance. The federal Constitution should be thought of not just as a legislative command but also as a judicial declaration, as a kind of precedent. And just as a court in jurisdiction A may often look to the precedents of sister courts in jurisdictions B, C, and D when it is adjudicating a case, a state court might look to the judicial statement of "we the people of the United States" sitting as a high court, as not just a sovereign legislature but a sovereign judiciary. We the people of the United States have declared that there is such a thing as *the* freedom of speech and *the* freedom of the press. This declaratory theory was embodied, in my view, in the Fourteenth Amendment.

The Fourteenth Amendment, I believe, was consciously designed to make applicable against the states various rights that were declared by the first eight amendments.[13] The declaratory theory of the Constitution, which was just a theory among antebellum lawyers, was by and large rejected in 1833 in *Barron* v. *Baltimore.* But it was embraced by those who framed and ratified the Fourteenth Amendment. That amendment was designed and widely understood to make applicable against the states those rights of citizens that had been declared in the federal Bill of Rights. The language in the Fourteenth Amendment that accomplishes this is not, as the Supreme Court has said, the Due Process Clause but rather the Privileges or Immunities Clause.

The Privileges or Immunities Clause self-consciously tracks the language of the First Amendment. The First Amendment says, "Congress shall make no law . . . abridging the freedom of speech, or of the press." *Shall, make, no, law, abridging.* And the Fourteenth Amendment says: "No state shall make or enforce any law which shall abridge the privileges or immunities of citizens of the United States." *No, shall, make, law, abridge.* This similar wording had a purpose: to underscore the connection between *the* privileges and immunities protected by the Fourteenth Amendment and *the* freedom of speech and *the* freedom of the press that had previously been declared by "we the people of the United States" in the First Amendment. Rights and freedoms declared in the federal Bill of Rights were widely understood as the paradigmatic privileges and immunities that no state would be able to abridge after the Fourteenth Amendment.

One final way to put that Fourteenth Amendment point is to embed it in a historical context.[14] The Abolitionists were centrally concerned about protecting free political expression, especially in the South. Before the Civil War, it was a crime in southern states to criticize slavery. It was a crime to teach blacks and to preach certain political ideas to them. Abolitionists were put in jail for preaching their political ideas. Their pamphlets were censored and withheld from the federal mail. A key purpose of Reconstruction Republicans was to open up free political expression, especially in the southern states. The Fourteenth Amendment would put an end to state censorship of political dissenters, and would protect freedom of speech and of the press against state action. This explicit theme was sounded again and again in the speeches of Reconstruction leaders in Congress like John Bingham, Jacob Howard, James Wilson, and Lyman Trumbull, and in state legislature after state legislature during the ratifying process. No Bill of Rights *privileges* or *immunities* or *rights* or *freedoms*—the same concepts are conveyed by all these terms—were affirmed more often in the Thirty-Ninth Congress than the freedoms of speech and press. (The only right that comes close is due process.)

Let us review the various arguments for why freedom of speech and freedom of the press are rights that legitimately apply against state governments as well as the federal government, and why incorporation of at least *these* rights is obviously correct. First, structural ideas about popular sovereignty. Second, textual embodiments of those ideas in the Preamble and the Republican Government Clause. Third, a declaratory reading of the First Amendment that goes beyond its federalism dimension of "Congress shall make no law" to its declaratory idea that certain rights exist, in particular *the* freedom of speech and *the* freedom of the press. Finally, and most importantly, the incorporation of that declaratory theory in the words and the spirit of the Fourteenth Amendment.

This brings us to the other side of the coin: "reverse incorporation," in which the federal government is obligated to abide by the same constitutional duty of equal protection that is imposed upon the states.

REVERSE INCORPORATION IN THE BOLLING CASE

By what right did the Supreme Court in the 1954 case *Bolling* v. *Sharpe* invalidate racial segregation perpetrated by the federal government?[15] *Bolling* was decided the same day as its companion case, *Brown* v. *Board of Education*.[16] *Brown* said that state-run segregated schools violated the Equal Protection Clause of the Fourteenth Amendment, and *Bolling* said that segregation in the federally run schools was also unconstitutional. But the Equal Protection Clause explicitly limits states, not the federal government. To the *Bolling* Court, this textual difference was largely irrelevant, as was federalism generally: "[I]t would be unthinkable that the same Constitution would impose a lesser duty on the Federal Government."[17]

Was *Bolling*'s "reverse incorporation" of equal-protection principles against the federal government sound? I think so; indeed, each of the arguments I have made for incorporation has a parallel of sorts in reverse incorporation.

Structural and Textual Arguments

First, just as we had a structural intuition about popular sovereignty, so we have one about race discrimination. Why is it at all legitimate in a republican government for government officials to stigmatize or degrade one caste or class of citizens? Why is that necessary or proper, to use the language of *McCulloch* v. *Maryland* and Article I, Section 8? What is the legitimate and *proper* purpose of segregation? Chief Justice Earl Warren's opinion in *Bolling* subtly invokes this Article I, Section 8, language: "Segregation in public education is not reasonably related to any *proper* governmental objective."[18] Note that I am assuming and asserting that the purpose of Jim Crow was to stigmatize and degrade. If equal-protection principles were not applicable to the federal government, the federal government would be able to pick out a group of people and stamp them inferior. Congress could pass a law entitled

"An Act to Degrade Blacks." What stops the government from doing that is a certain theory of equal protection.

To put it differently: any stigmatization of that sort is arguably an impermissible Bill of Attainder—a law aimed at a particular person or group—and the Constitution explicitly bars both the federal government (in Article I, Section 9) and the states (in Article I, Section 10) from passing such bills. The purpose of this prohibition is precisely to prevent the legislature—any legislature—from imposing a punishment or stigmatic harm on one caste or class of people. Consider also the Attainder Clauses' close cousins that bar both federal and state governments from passing *ex post facto* laws. Penal laws must punish persons, not for doing something that only later became legally wrong, but for doing something that was legally wrong when they did it. Such laws must be *prospective,* in that they announce a standard that will be enforced, thereby giving potential miscreants the opportunity to mend their ways. But many Jim Crow laws were designed to stigmatize blacks simply for who they were, which was certainly not something they could change.

Perhaps in the nineteenth century many people thought it was all right for the federal government to pass racially based laws but they would have denied that the purpose of those laws was to stigmatize one class of people. Today, the nineteenth-century logic that was used to uphold those laws no longer applies. The logic of *Plessy* v. *Ferguson* (1896) was that segregation was all right as long as it created truly equal situations for blacks and whites. *Brown* v. *Board of Education* responded that it was a simple empirical fact—indeed, I would say it was an undeniable fact to any honest person in 1954[19]—that the situations of blacks and whites under segregation were not truly equal. The purpose of Jim Crow laws was to dominate, degrade, and stigmatize one class of United States citizens, a subgroup of "we the people."

And blacks have indeed been part of "we the people" from the beginning. Slaves, perhaps, were not. But Chief Justice Roger Taney in *Dred Scott* got his history absolutely wrong when he implied that free blacks were not a central part of the founding experience. They voted in many state conventions, and they bore arms for their country. In his famous dissent in *Dred Scott,* Justice Benjamin Curtis proved that free blacks had been part of "we the people of the United States" from the founding.[20]

So I have now made a founding argument on the basis of an intuition—that a system designed to degrade a subclass of "we the people" cannot be necessary and proper, cannot be legitimate. I have given a textual basis for this intuition in the original Constitution, namely the Attainder Clause (with a little help from its *ex post facto* cousin). Now I will try to show how the Reconstruction experience underscores that intuition and gives us decisive additional support for the idea.

Support From Reconstruction

The Thirteenth Amendment abolishes slavery forever. It has no state action requirement. It applies to the federal government as well as to the states. The Thirteenth Amendment is all about affirming the equal citizenship of a previously degraded caste. I would argue that any kind of invidious segregation on the basis of race in America, or any other discrimination or unfavorable treatment that disadvantages people simply because they have dark skin, is a "badge" of servitude and therefore a violation of the spirit of the Thirteenth Amendment. The Thirteenth Amendment, to reiterate, does not apply only to the states—it applies to the federal government as well. It simply says, "Neither slavery nor involuntary servitude . . . shall exist within the United States. . . ." Jim Crow laws were a vestige of slavery. That is just a straight Thirteenth Amendment argument. Thus, in the Thirty-Ninth Congress, Senator Lyman Trumbull proclaimed—before the Fourteenth Amendment had even been proposed, much less ratified—that "any statute which is not equal to all" was "in fact, a badge of servitude which, by the Constitution, is prohibited."[21] By the way, Justice John Marshall Harlan, the great dissenter in *Patterson,* understood this Thirteenth Amendment argument and trumpeted it in his famous dissents in the *Civil Rights Cases*[22] and *Plessy* v. *Ferguson.*[23]

Now consider the Fourteenth Amendment. Its first sentence has no state action requirement. It affirms that all persons—blacks as well as whites—who are born in the United States are *citizens* of the United States. One thing that citizenship should mean, at the very least, is that citizens shall not be singled out for degradation and stigmatization merely because of their race. That understanding of the meaning of *citizen* is to be found throughout the Reconstruction era. So the Citizenship Clause of the Fourteenth Amendment has no state action requirement; it binds the federal government as well as the states, and it is a bar against certain kinds of stigmatization that deny equal citizenship. In the *Civil Rights Cases,* Justice Harlan declared that if citizenship entailed nothing else, it assuredly entailed "exemption from race discrimination in respect of any civil right belonging to citizens of the white race."[24] As he put the point in a later opinion, "All citizens are equal before the law."[25]

The second sentence of the Fourteenth Amendment says that a citizen has certain privileges and immunities. They are not created or conferred by the Fourteenth Amendment; they are *declared* there. The theory was that they preexist. So just as *the* freedom of speech and of the press in the First Amendment was a matter of a preexisting right that was not limited to Congress, so the affirmation in the Privileges or Immunities Clause that citizens have certain privileges and immunities is not limited to the states—it has implications for the federal government as well.

In *Plessy,* Justice Harlan, who would vigorously champion incorporation over the next dozen years in cases like *Patterson,*[26] elegantly identified this declaratory linkage between incorporation and reverse incorporation, celebrating "the clear, distinct, unconditional recognition by our governments, *National and State,* of every right that inheres in civil freedom [i.e., incorporation], and of the equality before the law of all citizens of the United States without regard to race [i.e., reverse incorporation]."[27]

Finally, let us move to the Due Process Clause. The language here, it might be thought, actually suggests a conscious intent to exclude equal protection as an idea applicable to the federal government. The Fifth Amendment talks about due process but does not mention equal protection, while the Fourteenth Amendment says that states cannot deny persons due process *or* equal protection. One might conclude, then, that equal protection is different from due process, and that only due process applies to the federal government (via the Fifth Amendment). But once we think about constitutional provisions as being declaratory, this kind of argument becomes deeply suspect. Just as it was a mistake to read "Congress" in the First Amendment in an *expressio unius* fashion so as to mean "Congress, but not states," so too it is a mistake to read "due process" in the Fifth Amendment to mean "due process, but not equal protection."

The mention of both due process and equal protection in the Fourteenth Amendment does not mean that there is no equal-protection idea implicit in due process in the Fifth Amendment. The Fourteenth Amendment distinguishes between two types of rights: the rights of *citizens,* who are entitled to privileges or immunities, and the rights of *persons,* who are entitled to equal protection and due process.[28] John Bingham and many others said that equal protection and due process are variations on the same idea.[29] He wrote in his original proposed Fourteenth Amendment, "Congress shall have power to make all laws which shall be necessary and proper to secure to the citizens of each State all privileges and immunities of citizens of the several States, and to all persons in the several States *equal protection* in the rights of *life, liberty, and property.*"[30] Bingham meshed together the equal-protection idea and the due-process right of life, liberty, and property. On the floor of the House he said, "Every word of this proposed amendment is today in the Constitution of our country,"[31] and no one challenged him on that. Howard Graham has shown that this rhetoric in Bingham goes back to as early as 1857.[32]

But Bingham is not unique in this; several state constitutions, from the founding on, meld the idea of equal protection and the idea of due process. The Pennsylvania Constitution of 1776, for example, speaks of how "every member of society hath a right to be protected in the enjoyment of life, liberty and property."[33] Similar affirmations appear also in the 1776 Delaware Declaration of Rights, the Vermont Constitution of 1777, the Massachusetts Constitution of 1780, and the New Hampshire Constitution of 1784[34] — and these examples are from just the founding period; I have not even begun to look at later state constitutions.

Consider next the classic definition of due process offered by Daniel Webster in his famous argument in the *Dartmouth College* case. Judge Thomas Cooley, in his influential nineteenth-century constitutional treatise,[35] would later say that "perhaps no definition [of due process] is more often quoted" than Webster's: due process means "due course and process of law," which means "law of the land," by which "is most clearly intended the general law. . . . The meaning is, that every citizen shall hold his life, liberty, and property, and immunities, under the protection of general rules."[36]

Although I have not yet completed my research, I am finding more and more historical support for a substantive meaning of due process, to the following extent: the framers of the Fourteenth Amendment tended to conflate due-process principles and equal-protection principles and to say that due process of *law,* at the very least, requires a general, non-discriminatory *law*—a requirement of generality that today we would articulate as rooted in the equal-protection principle.[37]

Justice Harlan, the great dissenter in *Plessy,* built that dissent in part upon an earlier opinion, where he had proclaimed that the "guarantees of life, liberty, and property are for all persons within the jurisdiction . . . without discrimination against any because of their race."[38] Note how this formulation marries due-process language ("life, liberty, and property") with equal-protection language ("all persons within the jurisdiction"—a phrase found only in the Equal Protection Clause) and equal-protection norms against race discrimination. Taken seriously, this marriage supports the reading of the Fifth Amendment's Due Process Clause as a ban on invidious race discrimination, as Harlan's very next sentence made clear: "Those guarantees . . . must be enforced in the Courts, *both of the Nation and of the State,* without reference to considerations based upon race."[39]

RIGHTS AND FEDERALISM

To sum up, let me identify the parallel structure of my arguments about incorporation and reverse incorporation. States should not be allowed to violate freedom of speech and of the press, first of all, because there was a basic structural intuition about popular sovereignty at the founding. We can find particular textual embodiments of that at the founding, in the Preamble and the Republican Guarantee Clause. We can even see some reflections of it in a declaratory reading of the First Amendment specifying an antecedent freedom of speech and of the press. Finally, and most importantly, that vision was absolutely at the center of the text and historical context of the Fourteenth Amendment.

Now, the parallel: the federal government should not be allowed to stigmatize on the basis of race; it should not be allowed to disadvantage blacks simply because of their race. This is a violation of the implicit equal citizenship of all. Why is it necessary and proper for the federal government to be in this race-stigmatization business? Isn't a stigmatization on the basis of race arguably a bill of attainder or *ex post facto* law that violates the norms of generality and prospectivity that are at the heart of a regime of law? (The bans on bills of attainder and *ex post facto* laws can thus also be understood as separation-of-powers ideas.) Finally, as with incorporation, this vision receives powerful endorsement from the Reconstruction vision: from the idea of the Thirteenth Amendment, which has no state action requirement; from the first sentence of the Fourteenth Amendment, the Citizenship Clause, which is an explicit affirmation of the equal-citizenship ideal; from the second sentence, the Privileges or Immunities Clause, which says that what it means to be a citizen is to have certain privileges and immunities, and that this declaration has consequences even against the federal government; and finally from the Due Process and Equal Protection clauses, which when read in a declaratory way actually tend to *equate,* rather than distinguish between, the concepts of equal protection and due process, and thereby gloss the Fifth Amendment due-process text. If the Fourteenth Amendment implies that due process and equal protection are two ways of saying the same thing, then we have to reread the Fifth Amendment's Due Process Clause as incorporating an equal-protection component.

To return, then, to where this discussion began: largely as a result of the declaratory theory (which, though a deviant theory at the founding, later undergirded the Fourteenth Amendment), federalism—so important in the definition of rights at the founding—seems to have virtually dropped out. The Fourteenth Amendment framers were really saying that rights should not vary so much between federal and state governments. People have rights, and once we find them they should limit all governments. The tricky thing is finding them.

The insight of the declaratory theory is that we can often look to the Constitution itself to help find rights, rather than looking elsewhere (philosophical treatises, the judicial conscience, and so on). The particular statement of these constitutional rights might be limited—they might be declared as rights against one government or another government—but the declaratory theory says: Read those statements not simply as affirmations of federalism but as declarations of rights, and when you read them that way they apply against both sets of governments. Where can you find a list of the "privileges" and "immunities" that no state shall abridge? Look first to those rights, freedoms, privileges, and immunities in the federal Bill of Rights! Where can you find the rights of "citizens" and "persons" that even the federal government may not violate? Look at the declaration of equal protection in the Fourteenth Amendment!

Federalism exists to serve rights, not to limit them.

5

The Right To Be Let Alone:
Constitutional Privacy in
Griswold, Roe, and *Bowers*

NADINE STROSSEN

Three major cases shaping the doctrine that is commonly labeled "constitutional privacy" are *Griswold* v. *Connecticut* (1965), in which the Supreme Court struck down a Connecticut statute that criminalized all use of contraceptives, including use by married persons; *Roe* v. *Wade* (1973), in which the Court struck down a Texas statute that criminalized all abortions, except for the purpose of saving the woman's life; and *Bowers* v. *Hardwick* (1986), in which the Court upheld a Georgia statute that criminalized all sodomy, broadly defined as any contact between the sex organs of one person and the mouth or anus of another person (without regard to gender, sexual orientation, or marital status).

Nadine Strossen is a professor of law at New York Law School and president of the American Civil Liberties Union (ACLU), which participated in all three cases discussed in this article. (In *Griswold* the ACLU filed *amicus* briefs in support of the parties asserting the constitutional privacy right; the ACLU represented the plaintiffs in *Roe*'s companion case, *Doe* v. *Bolton;* and in *Bowers* the ACLU represented plaintiff Michael Hardwick.) For research help with this article, the author thanks her ACLU assistants, Thomas Hilbink and Catherine Siemann, and NYLS student Carl Wistreich.

These cases do not concern "privacy" in the usual sense. Rather, in the constitutional context, "privacy" refers to the right of individuals to make certain personal choices in the realm of sexual relationships, familial relationships, and child-bearing. A term such as "autonomy" or "self-determination" would more aptly denote this right.

Griswold, Roe, and *Bowers* have been among the most widely discussed constitutional law cases, not just among legal scholars and other professional Supreme Court watchers but also among the general public. For example, during the spring of 1992, in anticipation of the Court's then forthcoming decision in *Planned Parenthood* v. *Casey*— which many expected would overturn *Roe* v. *Wade*— the May 2 issue of *Time* Magazine bore this cover caption: "Why *Roe* v. *Wade* Is Already Moot." During the televised Senate Judiciary Committee hearings on the Supreme Court nomination of Robert Bork in 1987, the *Griswold* case became a focal point, prompting Senator Arlen Specter to call it "the most discussed case in America." (In contrast, during the more recent hearings on the Supreme Court nomination of Clarence Thomas, *Roe* became conspicuous as—in terms of the nominee himself—probably the least discussed case!)

Precisely because these cases have occasioned so much commentary, it is refreshing to go back to the original Supreme Court decisions themselves. This trilogy of cases includes an unusually high number of separate opinions: six each in *Griswold* and *Roe,* and five in *Bowers,* for a total of seventeen. The discussions in these opinions incorporate and reiterate every major interpretive debate that had previously occurred in the Court's constitutional rulings, including: the natural-law debate between Justices Chase and Iredell in *Calder* v. *Bull,*[1] the substantive-due-process debate involved in cases decided during the *Lochner* era and its aftermath,[2] and the "incorporation" controversy about the extent to which the Fourteenth Amendment's Due Process Clause made provisions in the Bill of Rights or other fundamental rights enforceable against state governments.[3]

Because this trio of major privacy cases presents so many interpretive issues, I will necessarily be quite selective, focusing on four basic issues that are raised by all three cases. I will outline these questions and my own conclusions about them at the outset, and then note them again as they arise in the context of particular opinions.

First, at what level of abstraction or generality should the Court operate in constitutional interpretation? That is, how literally or abstractly should it read relevant constitutional provisions, past decisions, and the facts and issues involved in the case before it? Because the Constitution is designed to preserve individual liberty,[4] I believe that its liberty-protecting language should be read at a high level of generality, to protect the most expansive conception of freedom. For the same reason, Supreme Court precedents that protect individual rights should be read broadly, as implementing principles that extend beyond the particular facts of the cases involved. Likewise, in resolving human-rights cases, the Court should not focus narrowly on the particular facts and issues presented but should consider them illustrative of broader patterns and themes in rights jurisprudence.

Second, what standard of review should the Court apply in weighing individual privacy rights against countervailing societal justifications for restricting them? Ultimately, this question poses a choice between a presumption in favor of individual privacy and one in favor of societal restrictions. This choice, in turn, entails a selection between competing political philosophies: as these terms are classically used, a "liberal" political philosophy presumptively favors individual liberty, while a "conservative" philosophy presumptively favors maintenance of the status quo. I believe that our Constitution reflects the former, a liberal philosophy favoring individual liberty.

Third, is there a principled distinction between *Lochner*-type substantive due process and the concept of privacy? In other words, does the judicial power to invalidate state legislation as inconsistent with the right of privacy necessarily encompass the judicial power to invalidate state legislation as inconsistent with "liberty of contract"? Or is there some coherent distinction between property rights, such as contractual freedom, and "personal" rights, such as privacy? If so, is there a justification for according more protection to personal rights than to property rights?

Constitutional jurisprudence currently draws a bright-line distinction between personal liberty and property rights. Certainly the right to practice one's chosen occupation is central to one's sense of self, and thus seems deeply "personal."[5] Yet, for most purposes, the current law treats occupational choice as a matter that belongs in the sphere of economics and property and hence is essentially beyond the pale of meaningful constitutional protection. The fundamental personal rights involved in the privacy cases are certainly among the most important human rights. Therefore, judicial protection of these privacy rights does not necessarily imply that other personal rights should receive as much protection. One could plausibly argue, for example, that the selection of one's sexual partners and practices and the decision whether to have a child are more intimate than one's occupational choice, and that "Big Brother" has less of a legitimate basis for interfering with these choices.

Fourth, do the privacy decisions give power to the judiciary that should be exercised instead by the legislative branch of government? In my view, this often asked question is a red herring, since the cases concern decisions that should not be made by *any* governmental body or official, but should be left to individuals.

GRISWOLD V. CONNECTICUT

Griswold[6] involved a Connecticut statute that made it a crime for anyone, including a married couple, to use contraceptives. The executive director and medical director of a Planned Parenthood clinic were convicted as accessories for prescribing contraceptives to married couples.

From the standpoint of constitutional interpretation, the two most interesting opinions in *Griswold* are Justice John Marshall Harlan's concurrence in the judgment and Justice Hugo Black's dissent. To some extent, these opinions incorporate the debate that these same two justices previously had waged during the "incorporation" controversy, about the scope of the Fourteenth Amendment's Due Process Clause. Harlan's opinion set forth a persuasive approach to interpreting the Constitution as ensuring unenumerated rights in general and the right of privacy in particular. Black harshly criticized that approach, but in my view Harlan effectively countered his criticism. I will outline the other opinions and then focus on those by Justices Harlan and Black.

For the Court: Justice Douglas

Justice William O. Douglas's opinion for the majority assiduously avoided any suggestion that the rationale for invalidating the Connecticut statute was related to substantive due process—i.e., derived from the general "liberty" protected in the Fourteenth Amendment's Due Process Clause.[7] Instead, he said that the right to privacy is "peripheral" and "penumbral" to, and "emanates from," various specific guarantees in the Bill of Rights: the First Amendment freedom of association, the Third Amendment (which protects against the quartering of soldiers in private homes), the Fourth Amendment (which protects against unwarranted and unreasonable searches and seizures), and the Fifth Amendment (which protects against compulsory self-incrimination).[8]

There were probably two reasons for Justice Douglas's refusal to ground the *Griswold* ruling in a substantive-due-process theory. First, the Court had definitively rejected this theory—at least in the context of laws affecting property rights—in *Ferguson* v. *Skrupa*[9] (decided by an 8-1 vote), just two years earlier. Second, Justice Douglas endorsed Justice Black's position in the incorporation controversy—namely, that the Fourteenth Amendment's Due Process Clause incorporates the specific guarantees in the Bill of Rights, and does not incorporate some general concept of fundamental fairness.[10] It was generally consistent with this approach to ground a constitutional privacy protection in specific Bill of Rights provisions. This aspect of the majority opinion was what prompted Justice Harlan to write a separate concurrence; he rejected the majority's suggestion that the Due Process Clause is coextensive with the letter or penumbra of the Bill of Rights, and he objected to this implicit limitation on the scope of the clause's "liberty" guarantee.[11]

Although Justice Douglas's majority opinion apparently recognized that government may theoretically limit constitutional privacy to some extent, it summarily concluded that the challenged statute constituted an overly broad restriction, emphasizing its intrusion into the time-honored marriage relationship:

> Would we allow the police to search the sacred precincts of marital bedrooms for telltale signs of the use of contraceptives? The very idea is repulsive to the notions of privacy surrounding the marriage relationship.[12]

> We deal with a right of privacy older than the Bill of Rights—older than our political parties, older than our school system. Marriage

is a coming together for better or for worse, hopefully enduring, and intimate to the degree of being sacred. It is an association that promotes a way of life, not causes; a harmony in living, not political faiths; a bilateral loyalty, not commercial or social projects. Yet it is an association for as noble a purpose as any involved in our prior decisions.[13]

This aspect of Justice Douglas's opinion has significant implications for our first broad issue of constitutional interpretation, i.e., to what extent the focus should be on particulars, whether constitutional provisions or the facts and holdings of judicial decisions. For those who seek to cabin the *Griswold* ruling, the foregoing passage's reference to privacy of two specific sorts could be read as confining the scope of the decision to those particular types of privacy: within a marital relationship, or within a home, where one is to be free from unwarranted government searches and seizures.

As we shall see later, in *Bowers* Justice Byron White stressed the marital and procreational context of *Griswold* to justify his narrow view of constitutional privacy. Accordingly, he rejected Michael Hardwick's argument that such privacy encompassed sexual intimacies more generally. Similarly, the Reagan Justice Department, in seeking to distinguish *Griswold* from *Roe* while urging the Court to overrule the latter only, argued that *Griswold* essentially protects individuals against physical searches of their homes.[14] Although some members of the Court apparently have accepted the former limitation on *Griswold*'s scope—its emphasis on the marriage relationship—no justice has endorsed the second proffered limitation.

Other Opinions

Justice Goldberg Concurs. In an opinion joined by Chief Justice Earl Warren and Justice William J. Brennan, Justice Arthur J. Goldberg endorsed the majority opinion. He nonetheless wrote separately, "to emphasize the relevance of [the Ninth] Amendment to the Court's holding."[15] Goldberg noted that the language of the Ninth Amendment ("The enumeration in the Constitution, of certain rights, shall not be construed to deny or disparage others retained by the people"), as well as its underlying history, reveals the Framers' belief that there were additional fundamental rights beyond those enumerated in the Bill of Rights.

Justice White Concurs. In contrast with the majority opinion's eschewal of the Due Process Clause, Justice Byron White based his concurrence in the judgment squarely on that provision. In his view, the Due Process Clause protects a "'realm of family life which the state cannot enter' without substantial justification."[16] White distinguished the *Lochner* line of substantive-due-process cases, which the Court had repudiated in *Ferguson* v. *Skrupa,* by emphasizing the importance of the marriage relationship and noting that marriage "'come[s] to this Court with a momentum for respect lacking when appeal is made to liberties which derive merely from shifting economic arrangements.'"[17]

As we shall see, Justice White's emphasis on the traditionally protected marriage relationship in his *Griswold* concurrence became critically significant for his majority opinion in *Bowers.* In the latter, White drew a sharp distinction between the challenged anti-sodomy statute and the factual situations involved in the Court's previous privacy cases—including *Griswold*—because the latter all concerned matters of marriage, family, and procreation.[18]

Justice Stewart Dissents. Justice Potter Stewart decried the Connecticut statute as "uncommonly silly"[19] but said that the Due Process Clause did not give the Court power to invalidate it. He read that clause, in light of the Court's abandonment of *Lochner* and its progeny, as securing only procedural due process.[20] As we shall see, Justice Stewart expressly recanted this narrow reading of the Due Process Clause eight years later, in his concurring opinion in *Roe.*

Justice Harlan Concurs. As previously noted, Justice John Marshall Harlan declined to join the Court's opinion because of one feature that it shared with the dissenting opinions: its implicit limitation on the scope of the "liberty" sheltered by the Due Process Clause as encompassing only those rights that are within the letter or penumbra of the Bill of Rights.[21] In other words, Justice Harlan's opinion in *Griswold* maintained the position he had asserted in the incorporation controversy: that the Due Process Clause embodies a concept of fundamental rights that does not necessarily extend to, and is not necessarily limited to, all the rights set forth in the Bill of Rights.[22] Accordingly, for Justice Harlan, the relevant question about the Connecticut statute in *Griswold* was the same one he had posed about other state statutes that had arguably violated specific Bill of Rights provisions: Did it "violate[ ] basic values 'implicit in the concept of ordered liberty'"?[23]

Justice Harlan concluded that the Connecticut statute did violate such basic values, for the reasons he had set forth in his dissent four years earlier in *Poe* v. *Ullman*.[24] There the Court had dismissed a challenge to the same Connecticut statute at issue in *Griswold* on the grounds that it was non-justiciable, i.e., not something that the Court could settle. Justice Harlan dissented from the Court's non-justiciability ruling, examined the claim, and concluded that the statute contravened the Due Process Clause.[25]

It is remarkable that the first Supreme Court opinion invalidating a prohibition against contraception under a privacy guarantee deemed implicit in the Due Process Clause was written by Justice John Marshall Harlan, a classic conservative jurist who epitomized qualities of judicial restraint. This shows how far Robert Bork was from the mainstream of constitutional interpretation—including the mainstream of judicial conservatism[26]—in his sharp criticism of *Griswold* and the implied constitutional right to privacy.[27]

I will return to Justice Harlan's important opinion in *Poe* v. *Ullman*, but first I want to outline Justice Black's dissent in *Griswold*, since Harlan's opinions in *Poe* and *Griswold* contain responses to Black's critiques of the *Griswold* ruling.

Justice Black Dissents. In terms of constitutional interpretation, this is an important opinion. Justice Black expressly linked his position in *Griswold* to every major past debate about constitutional interpretation that the Court had undertaken.[28] For example, he quoted at length from Justice Iredell's opinion in *Calder* v. *Bull*,[29] rejecting the natural-law approach to constitutional interpretation. He also quoted an extended passage from his own dissent in *Adamson* v. *California*,[30] rejecting the natural-law approach to the incorporation controversy. Finally, he invoked the fear of *Lochner* and the substantive-due-process era. Justice Black's sharpest disagreement was not with the majority opinion but rather with the concurring opinions, precisely because of the interpretive approaches they espoused.

Along with his fellow dissenter, Justice Stewart, Justice Black vigorously stressed his disagreement with the Connecticut law as a policy matter.[31] He characterized his disagreement with the majority opinion as relatively narrow, because he shared the majority's view that the law could, in principle, violate the First Amendment. Accordingly, Black's difference with the majority was only as to whether, on this set of facts, the First Amendment was indeed violated.[32]

Black's disagreement with the concurring justices was more fundamental. Unlike them, he did not believe that the Due Process Clause or the Ninth Amendment could ever, under any circumstances, be a proper basis for invalidating legislation. This aspect of Black's opinion reiterated interpretive positions he had consistently asserted in the incorporation cases.[33] As interpreted by Justices Harlan and Goldberg, the Due Process Clause and the Ninth Amendment would give the federal judiciary, in Black's words, "power to invalidate any legislative acts which the judges find irrational, unreasonable, or offensive."[34] Justice Black deplored this "natural law due process philosophy,"[35] which he said is more like law-making than law-interpreting.

Echoing an oft-repeated refrain during the incorporation debates, Black objected to Harlan's "fundamental rights" approach to defining the scope of the Due Process Clause by noting that the Court has no mechanism for determining which principles are fundamental: "Our Court certainly has no machinery with which to take a Gallup Poll."[36] He also stated that the Court's use of loose, flexible standards to invalidate state laws endangered principles of federalism and of separation of powers.

Just as he relied on other past controversies about constitutional interpretation, Justice Black also invoked the specter of the discredited rulings during the *Lochner* era, arguing that the defects and dangers in those decisions were being revived by the *Griswold* ruling. He said that the *Lochner* approach had threatened the nation's tranquillity and stability, and that natural-justice concepts are "no less dangerous when used to enforce this Court's views about personal rights than when used to enforce its views about economic rights."[37] Finding no principled distinction between the concept of fundamental rights or natural justice in the *Lochner* context and in the constitutional-privacy context, Black said it was only a fortuity that the judicial-review power wielded in *Griswold* was not there used to invalidate state economic regulations—a fortuity based on the personal predilections of the current justices rather than on some neutral constitutional principle:

Apparently my Brethren have less quarrel with state economic regulations than former Justices of their persuasion [i.e., believing in substantive due process] had. But any limitation upon their using the natural law due process philosophy to strike down any state law, dealing with any activity whatever, will obviously be only self-imposed.[38]

Black's Approach v. Harlan's Approach

Justice Black said that the only possible basis for invalidating a state law is an express constitutional provision. This literalistic approach was most tellingly expressed in the following statement:

I like my privacy as well as the next one, but I am nevertheless compelled to admit that government has a right to invade it unless prohibited by some specific constitutional provision.[39]

From Black's perspective, there is a presumption of government power unless the Constitution expressly limits that power. Justice Harlan takes the opposite approach: in his view, there is a presumption of individual liberty unless the Constitution expressly gives the government power to limit it. Harlan's opinion in *Poe* v. *Ullman,* for example, reveals this alternative vision:[40]

[T]he full scope of the liberty guaranteed by the Due Process Clause cannot be . . . limited by the precise terms of the specific guarantees elsewhere . . . in the Constitution. This "liberty" is not a series of isolated points pricked out in terms of the taking of property; the freedom of speech, press, and religion; the right to keep and bear arms; the freedom from unreasonable searches and seizures; and so on. It is a rational continuum which, broadly speaking, includes a freedom from all substantial arbitrary impositions and purposeless restraints. . . .

The contrast between Black's presumption of governmental power and Harlan's presumption of individual liberty, in interpreting the Constitution, was aptly described in a metaphor that Professor Stephen Macedo used to describe two other persons.[41] To borrow his metaphor and apply it to Justices Harlan and Black: Harlan perceived the Constitution as creating islands of government authority amidst a sea of individual freedom, whereas Black perceived the Constitution as creating islands of individual freedom amidst a sea of government authority.

In other respects, too, Justice Harlan's opinion in *Griswold*—as well as his opinion in *Poe,* which it incorporated—contrasts with Black's interpretive approach. These Harlan opinions constitute classic statements of an approach to constitutional interpretation regarding issues of individual rights, including privacy, that is appropriately protective of such rights. In *Poe,* Harlan eschewed the literalistic constitutional interpretation that Black advocated in *Griswold;* Harlan said, instead, that the Court should approach the constitutional text "not in a literalistic way, as if we had a tax statute before us, but as the basic charter of our society, setting out in spare but meaningful terms the principles of government."[42] This is of course a restatement of Chief Justice John Marshall's famous "Constitution expounding" language in *McCulloch* v. *Maryland,*[43] which Harlan cites.[44]

The presumption that informed Harlan's interpretive perspective —that rights are secured unless government is expressly granted power to restrict them—arises from the view that a chief purpose of the government established under the U.S. Constitution is to secure fundamental rights. Citing *Calder* v. *Bull,*[45] Harlan expressed this natural-rights understanding of the Constitution's intent as follows:

> Through the course of this Court's decisions, [due process] has represented the balance which our Nation, *built upon postulates of respect for the liberty of the individual,* has struck between that liberty and the demands of organized society.[46]

In addition to this general interpretive and philosophical difference from Black, Harlan rejected Black's reading of the Due Process Clause for one specific textual reason: the fact that the Bill of Rights itself contains a due-process clause—in the Fifth Amendment—proved to Harlan that the Fourteenth Amendment's Due Process Clause is an independent guarantee, "more general and inclusive than the specific prohibitions."[47] From this perspective, if the Fourteenth Amendment's Due Process Clause could be read as incorporating all the rights guaranteed in the Bill of Rights, then the Fifth Amendment's Due Process Clause would be subject to a like interpretation; but if so, the other Bill of Rights provisions would be rendered superfluous.

Therefore, this argument went, on the assumption that the other Bill of Rights guarantees are not merely redundant of those implicit in the Due Process Clause, the Due Process Clause itself must secure freedoms other than those in the Bill of Rights.

A possible answer to this argument is that the Due Process Clause guarantees only *procedural* fairness, and is not a repository of unenumerated substantive rights. Under that reading, the Fifth Amendment's Due Process Clause would still be saved from redundancy, but there would be no license for enforcing "fundamental rights" against the states under the Fourteenth Amendment's Due Process Clause. Harlan rejected this narrow reading of the latter clause, though, by noting that the Court had long ago dismissed the notion that it guarantees procedural fairness only.[48] Even Justice Rehnquist, in his dissent in *Roe* v. *Wade,* agreed that the Due Process Clause goes beyond procedural fairness and protects some unenumerated rights; his only quarrel with the majority was the degree of protection that should be afforded those rights.[49] Likewise, as we shall see, having asserted in *Griswold* that the Due Process Clause secures only procedural fairness, Justice Stewart expressly recanted that position in *Roe.*[50]

Thus there is indeed a judicial consensus that the Due Process Clause embraces some substantive human-rights protections, even among justices who have sharp disagreements both about constitutional interpretation generally and about the precise scope of the Due Process Clause specifically. Consequently, there is apparently a judicial consensus accepting the textual argument for Harlan's fundamental-rights interpretation of the Fourteenth Amendment's Due Process Clause.

In his *Griswold* and *Poe* opinions, Justice Harlan forcefully made the case for a broad reading not only of the Due Process Clause but also of all constitutional provisions guaranteeing individual liberty. In contrast with the literalistic reading espoused by Justice Black, Harlan believed that these provisions should be construed at higher levels of abstraction. Accordingly, Harlan examined the broad purposes underlying explicit textual provisions and extrapolated from them additional protections consistent with such purposes. This broad, contextual approach to constitutional interpretation was best described in the following passage from Harlan's opinion in *Poe:*

The character of constitutional provisions . . . must be discerned from a particular provision's larger context. And inasmuch as this context is one not [only] of words, but [also] of history and purposes, the full scope of the liberty guaranteed by the Due Process Clause cannot be found in or limited by the precise terms of the specific guarantees elsewhere provided in the Constitution.[51]

This approach was also well described by another passage in the same vein:

It is the purposes of those guarantees and not their text, the reasons for their statement by the Framers and not the statement itself, which have led to their present status in the compendious notion of "liberty" embraced in the Fourteenth Amendment.[52]

Harlan's approach to constitutional interpretation is consistent with Douglas's penumbral approach in the *Griswold* majority, since it too derived broader protections from the underlying purposes and overarching themes that unified specific guarantees. In contrast, Stewart's dissent criticized the majority's analysis by arguing that the specific constitutional provisions containing particular privacy rights should be construed narrowly and concretely. Accordingly, Stewart dismissed the Third and Fourth Amendments as utterly irrelevant to the Connecticut statute at issue in *Griswold:* "No soldier has been quartered in any house. There has been no search, and no seizure."[53]

Under this view, the Constitution's delineation of a series of particular privacy rights, in specific contexts, belies the existence of a more comprehensive, generalized right. This cramped view of constitutional interpretation is fully answered by Harlan's language in *Poe,* which I quoted earlier, about the necessity of viewing these specific rights not in isolation but as elements of a larger pattern.[54] In that vein, he said the following specifically about the Third and Fourth Amendments:

It would surely be an extreme instance of sacrificing substance to form were it to be held that the constitutional principle of privacy against arbitrary official intrusion comprehends only physical invasions by the police. To be sure, the times presented the Framers with two particular threats to that principle, the general warrant . . . and the quartering of soldiers in private homes. But though

"Legislation, both statutory and constitutional, is enacted . . . from an experience of evils, . . . its general language should not, therefore, be necessarily confined to the form that evil had theretofore taken. . . . A principle to be vital must be capable of wider application than the mischief which gave it birth."[55]

Harlan criticized Black's understanding of the Fourteenth Amendment's Due Process Clause as protecting no freedoms beyond those in the Bill of Rights, not only for the foregoing reasons stemming from his contrasting philosophy of constitutional interpretation, but also because he believed Black's understanding was inconsistent with the history giving rise to the Fourteenth Amendment. Therefore, in Harlan's view, Black's construction ultimately was grounded only in a desire to constrain judicial discretion.[56]

As a preeminent practitioner of judicial conservatism, Harlan certainly agreed that judicial self-restraint is important as a goal. However, he did not regard Black's reading of the Due Process Clause as a necessary or sufficient means for achieving that goal. It was not *sufficient,* he maintained, because the explicit language in the Bill of Rights is also subject to subjective interpretations. For a recent example, Harlan cited the reapportionment cases, in which he had vigorously dissented from the majority's reading of the Equal Protection Clause as mandating the redrawing of legislative boundaries to guarantee "one person, one vote."[57] Harlan also contended that Black's reading of the Due Process Clause was not a *necessary* means for achieving judicial self-restraint because that goal could be attained through other means, including respect for history, adherence to the basic values that underlie our society, and compliance with principles of federalism and of separation of powers.

ROE V. WADE

In *Roe* v. *Wade*[58] the Supreme Court invalidated a Texas statute that criminalized all abortions except those performed for the purpose of saving the woman's life. The plaintiffs had argued that the constitutional right of privacy should be grounded in any or all of the constitutional provisions that had been cited in the various *Griswold* opinions: the Due Process Clause; specific provisions in the Bill of Rights and their penumbras; and the Ninth Amendment.

For the Court: Justice Blackmun

Justice Harry A. Blackmun's majority opinion treated the constitutional source of the privacy right in a fairly offhanded fashion. He did not discuss this issue at all but rather asserted in passing the existence of *some* constitutionally rooted privacy right, as a given:

> This right of privacy, whether it be founded in the Fourteenth Amendment's concept of personal liberty and restrictions upon state action, as we feel it is, or, as the District Court determined, in the Ninth Amendment's reservation of rights to the people, is broad enough to encompass a woman's decision whether or not to terminate her pregnancy.[59]

In the ongoing and vitriolic debate about *Roe,* its most often overlooked aspect is its moderate approach. Its detractors insistently repeat that *Roe* is an "extreme" decision, guaranteeing "abortion on demand." But it does no such thing. This is the primary point of Chief Justice Warren E. Burger's concurrence, which noted that the dissenters exaggerated the scope of the majority opinion: "Plainly, the Court today rejects any claim that the Constitution requires abortions on demand."[60]

The *Roe* plaintiffs had contended, as do some "pro-choice" advocates today, that terminating a pregnancy should be absolutely within a woman's prerogative, at any point prior to live birth, for any reason. Blackmun's opinion, though, twice expressly rejected this argument.[61] Conversely, the State of Texas contended, as do some "pro-life" advocates today, that abortion should be absolutely prohibited from the moment of conception on, unless it is necessary to save the woman's life. Blackmun's opinion also expressly rejected this position. Justice Blackmun adopted a moderate course, steering clear of the extremes offered by the contending parties.

Other Opinions

Justice Stewart Concurs. While the majority opinion did not include any discussion of the Due Process Clause rationale that it endorsed

in passing, Justice Potter Stewart's concurrence unabashedly characterized the majority's stance—and even the ruling in *Griswold*—as a
return to substantive due process. As noted above, Stewart had dissented in *Griswold* precisely because he then opposed what he viewed
as *Griswold*'s misguided resuscitation of substantive due process. In
Roe, though, Stewart repudiated his *Griswold* dissent and endorsed
what he considered to be a continuing line of cases grounded in
substantive due process:

> In 1963, in *Ferguson* v. *Skrupa,* this Court purported to sound the
> death knell for the doctrine of substantive due process, . . . under
> which many state laws had . . . been held to violate the Fourteenth
> Amendment. . . .
>
> Barely two years later, in *Griswold . . . ,* the Court held a Con-
> necticut birth control law unconstitutional. In view of what had
> been so recently said, the Court's opinion in *Griswold* understand-
> ably did its best to avoid reliance on the Due Process Clause of the
> Fourteenth Amendment. . . . Yet, the Connecticut law did not vio-
> late any provision of the Bill of Rights, nor any other specific
> provision of the Constitution. So it was clear to me then, and it is
> equally clear to me now, that . . . *Griswold* . . . can be rationally
> understood only as a holding that the Connecticut statute substan-
> tively invaded the "liberty" that is protected by the Due Process
> Clause of the Fourteenth Amendment. As so understood, *Griswold*
> stands as one in a long line of pre-*Skrupa* cases decided under the
> doctrine of substantive due process, and I now accept it as such.[62]

Justice Douglas Concurs. The author of the *Griswold* majority opinion
rejected Justice Stewart's characterization of that opinion as part of
the *Lochner*ian tradition of substantive due process. In his *Roe* concurrence, Justice William O. Douglas argued that there is a material
distinction between the Court's abandonment of substantive due
process in the economic and social sphere—i.e., its refusal to engage
in strict scrutiny of laws regulating economic and social conditions—
and its affirmation of substantive due process in the context of privacy
—i.e., its subjecting laws that intrude on privacy to strict scrutiny.
Essentially, the asserted distinction was the one that Douglas had
posited in *Griswold* itself: that privacy rights are more fundamental,
more important, than property rights.[63]

Douglas's argument on this point was essentially identical to that made by Justice White in *Griswold*—a fact that demonstrates the subjective nature of these determinations. For Justice White, it is apparently clear that the marital relationship deserves "respect" that is not due to economic relationships,[64] but it is equally clear that the woman's interest in not carrying a pregnancy to term, which was at stake in *Roe,* does not deserve such respect, nor does the interest of adults in engaging in certain kinds of sexual intimacy, which was at stake in *Bowers.* For Justice Blackmun, however, all the interests presented by all of these cases deserved sufficiently heightened respect to trigger strict judicial scrutiny of government restrictions on them. Yet another set of conclusions about the relative importance of these various asserted rights was reached by Justice Burger, who accorded heightened respect to the individual interests at issue in *Griswold* and *Roe* but not to those involved in *Bowers.*

As Justice Black indicated in his *Griswold* dissent, this kind of hierarchical ranking, in determining whether a right is sufficiently fundamental to be deemed implicitly protected against any governmental infringement, rests on the same types of value judgments that are involved in deciding whether a right is sufficiently fundamental to be deemed incorporated in the Fourteenth Amendment's Due Process Clause and hence protected against state governmental infringement. Thus, Black assailed both types of determinations as purely discretionary and subjective.

The rigid dichotomy that the Court has drawn between property and personal rights troubles me, for two reasons. First, it is hard to draw a principled distinction between these types of rights.[65] An individual (and the Court) may consider an economic or property interest to be an important personal right. Additionally, an economic right may be inextricably linked to a personal right, in that the former is an essential prerequisite for meaningfully exercising the latter. The Supreme Court itself noted the oversimplified nature of this distinction in *Lynch* v. *Household Finance Corporation:*

> The dichotomy between personal liberties and property rights is a false one. Property does not have rights. People have rights. The right to enjoy property without unlawful deprivation, no less than the right to speak or the right to travel, is in truth a "personal"

right, whether the "property" in question be a welfare check, a home, or a savings account. In fact, a fundamental interdependence exists between the personal right to liberty and the personal right in property. Neither could have meaning without the other.[66]

Second, from a pragmatic or strategic viewpoint, the Court's lessened protection of property rights, which it introduced in the cases overturning *Lochner* et al., has from the beginning posed a threat to personal rights—namely, that the cases in the former category would be used as precedents for cases in the latter category. Indeed, in the past few years, that potential danger has become an actual one; the Court has increasingly been subjecting government infringements on classic personal liberties to the kind of deferential, low-level scrutiny that it previously had applied only to infringements on property rights, with the result that such infringements are virtually automatically upheld.[67]

Since the two-tiered approach to personal and property rights that Justice Douglas defended in his *Roe* concurrence was shared by other justices—indeed, that approach was then and still is the prevailing constitutional orthodoxy—a more important feature of his *Roe* concurrence is its clear articulation of an affirmative theory of privacy as an aspect of liberty and autonomy. Douglas laid out a vision of constitutional privacy not only as the negative "right to be let alone" but also as a positive right. This affirmative perspective was implicit in Blackmun's majority opinion, but it was clearly set out in Douglas's concurrence.

Justice Douglas agreed with the dissenters in *Griswold* and *Roe* that the Ninth Amendment does not *create* any federally enforceable rights, but he echoed Goldberg's view in *Griswold* that it is an interpretive tool, affording textual recognition of the fact that constitutional protection extends to fundamental rights that are not enumerated in the Constitution itself.[68] Douglas also believed that the same purpose was served by the reference in the Constitution's Preamble to "the Blessings of Liberty," stating that it "includes customary, traditional, and time-honored rights, amenities, privileges, and immunities. . . . Many of them, in my view, come within the meaning of the term 'liberty' as used in the Fourteenth Amendment."[69]

Douglas then outlined three basic rights that—consistent with the

Ninth Amendment and the Preamble—he believed to be encompassed within the Due Process Clause's notion of "liberty":

> First is the autonomous control over the development and expression of one's intellect, interests, tastes, and personality. . . .
>
> Second is freedom of choice in the basic decisions of one's life respecting marriage, divorce, procreation, contraception, and the education and upbringing of children.
>
> Third is the freedom to care for one's health and person, freedom from bodily restraint or compulsion, freedom to walk, stroll or loaf.[70]

Douglas's affirmative conception of constitutional privacy underscores the point that "privacy" is somewhat of a misnomer for a concept that could more accurately be labeled "autonomy" or "self-determination," since it designates an individual's right to make choices about important personal matters. This broader, positive notion of privacy is well stated in a passage from *Jacobson v. Massachusetts*, which Douglas quoted:

> There is . . . a sphere within which the individual may assert the supremacy of his own will and rightfully dispute the authority of any human government,—especially of any free government existing under a written constitution, to interfere with the exercise of that will.[71]

While Blackmun's majority opinion in *Roe* endorsed an affirmative concept of liberty-as-autonomy only implicitly, Blackmun's ringing dissent in *Bowers* explicitly echoed and carried forward this concept, in the spirit of Douglas's *Roe* concurrence. Blackmun's *Bowers* dissent urged not only that the state should not interfere with cloistered sexuality in the privacy of the home, but also that the Constitution affirmatively protects different forms of sexual intimacy as central to self-realization.[72]

Some feminist legal theorists have highly praised Douglas's concurrence in *Roe* because they believe it heralded their own concerns that traditional constitutional privacy doctrine may afford too narrow a grounding for reproductive freedom.[73] Some feminist theorists have commented that the right of privacy is a passive right, merely forbidding the state from intervening in individual lives, whereas an affirmative concept of reproductive freedom implies that the state has an affirmative obligation to ensure that women actually exercise such freedom.[74] Consistent with this feminist outlook, Douglas's opinion emphasized the concrete harms that women suffered if they could not get abortions,[75] and his affirmative theory of autonomy supported the notion that women should be agents of their own lives.

Justice White Dissents. In contrast with Justice Douglas's emphasis on the significant harms suffered by women denied access to abortions, Justice Byron R. White's dissent in *Roe* repeatedly trivialized what is at stake for women. No fewer than four times in his opinion, White dismissed the decision to have an abortion as a mere matter of the woman's "convenience," and also characterized this choice as a "whim" or "caprice."[76] Moreover, he asserted that the majority catered to mere concerns of convenience or even caprice by guaranteeing abortion on demand:

> At the heart of the controversy . . . are those recurring pregnancies that pose no danger whatsoever to the life or health of the mother but are, nevertheless, unwanted for any one or more of a variety of reasons—convenience, family planning, economics, dislike of children, the embarrassment of illegitimacy, etc. The claim is that for any one of such reasons, or for no reason at all, any woman is entitled to an abortion at her request. . . . The Court for the most part sustains this position: pre-viability, [it] values the convenience, whim, or caprice of the pregnant woman more than the life or potential life of the fetus.[77]

Justice White took exactly the same tack in his majority opinion in *Bowers:* there, as in *Roe,* he grossly trivialized the individual right at stake by focusing on its most controversial, unpopular manifestations. In *Roe,* Justice White ignored the fact that Texas prohibited abortions that were sought even for such widely supported reasons as protecting the woman's health. Instead, he focused only on abortions that might be chosen for less compelling, and less widely supported, reasons. Likewise, as we shall see, in his *Bowers* opinion White ignored the fact that Georgia's anti-sodomy law criminalized certain forms of sexual intimacy even when they were practiced voluntarily by married heterosexual couples in the privacy of their own homes. Instead, he focused on sexual intimacies between unmarried gay men, thus playing upon society's homophobia.

White's dissent in *Roe* also foreshadowed his majority opinion in *Bowers* in a second respect: its castigation of the exercise of judicial power regarding matters that he believed should be left to the political branches of government. In *Roe*, White assailed the majority's ruling as "an exercise of raw judicial power" and "an improvident and extravagant exercise of the power of judicial review."[78] Likewise, in *Bowers,* White justified his narrow view of fundamental rights, including privacy, in terms of the constrained role he believed courts should play. He said, for example, that the Court should not take an expansive view of its authority "to discover new fundamental rights embedded in the Due Process Clause," explaining:

> The Court is most vulnerable and comes nearest to illegitimacy when it deals with judge-made constitutional law having little or no cognizable roots in the language or design of the Constitution.[79]

In support of this generalization, White referred to the "constitutional crisis" associated with the *Lochner* era and its repudiation.[80]

Before turning to a more detailed analysis of *Bowers,* I would like to examine one aspect of the other dissent in *Roe.*

Justice Rehnquist Dissents. As noted above, Justice William H. Rehnquist expressly agreed with the majority that the Due Process Clause protects unenumerated rights, but disagreed about the extent of that protection. Specifically, Rehnquist completely rejected heightened judicial scrutiny under a Due Process Clause analysis; he argued that this form of judicial review was appropriate only in an Equal Protection Clause analysis.[81]

This narrow perspective on the availability of non-deferential judicial review is consistent with Rehnquist's general majoritarian orientation. In his view, the Court should essentially rubber-stamp the decisions of the elected branches of government, even when they invade the rights of individuals or minority groups.[82] His proffered justification for that view is that the weighing of competing individual rights and majoritarian concerns is more appropriately done by the legislative, rather than the judicial, branch of government.[83]

The flaw in Rehnquist's cramped view of the judicial role is its disregard of the fact that judges (at least at the federal level) are uniquely situated to withstand majoritarian pressures that threaten rights of individuals and minority groups. To relegate such rights to the elected branches of government, as Rehnquist advocates, is to deprive them of the security that the Bill of Rights intended them to have.[84] This perspective, which is a constant theme throughout our constitutional history, was nowhere more powerfully expressed than in Justice Robert H. Jackson's eloquent majority opinion in *West Virginia Board of Education* v. *Barnette:*

> The very purpose of the Bill of Rights [and of the Court in enforcing it] was to remove certain rights from the vicissitudes of political controversy, to place them beyond the reach of majorities and officials and to establish them as legal principles to be applied by the courts. One's . . . fundamental rights may not be submitted to a vote; they depend on the outcome of no elections.[85]

Justice Rehnquist's rejection of the Court's special role as enforcer of the Bill of Rights is particularly puzzling in light of his apparent recognition that the Court *does* have a special role in enforcing the Equal Protection Clause. His *Roe* dissent expressly acknowledged that strict judicial scrutiny is appropriate in the latter context.[86] Why does Rehnquist believe that equality rights, but not rights of free speech, religious freedom, and the others secured through the Bill of Rights (and now enforceable against state and local governments through the Fourteenth Amendment's Due Process Clause), deserve the enhanced protection resulting from heightened judicial scrutiny of measures encroaching on them?

For the reasons set forth above, Justice Rehnquist's deferential approach to liberty-infringing measures, espoused in his *Roe* dissent, is both internally inconsistent and at odds with longstanding constitutional and judicial traditions. Nevertheless, in the years since *Roe,* this majoritarian approach has increasingly tended to color not only Rehnquist's dissenting opinions but also, and more frequently, majority opinions written by him or by one of his colleagues who share this orientation.[87] *Bowers* v. *Hardwick* exemplifies this unfortunate trend.

THE RIGHT TO BE LET ALONE   109

BOWERS V. HARDWICK

In *Bowers*,[88] the Court upheld a Georgia statute that criminalized all acts of sodomy, regardless of where they occurred and who engaged in them. Thus, consensual sodomy between a husband and wife, in the privacy of their home, was fully as unlawful as sodomy between homosexual males in a public place. For each such act, the Georgia statute authorized imprisonment of from one to twenty years.

The plaintiff, Michael Hardwick, was arrested after a police officer watched him having oral sex with another adult male in a bedroom of his own house. The officer, who had been admitted to the house by Hardwick's roommate, entered the bedroom unnoticed and un-announced and watched Hardwick's sexual encounter for about thirty-five seconds before arresting him. He also refused to leave the bedroom while the two men got dressed, stating, "I have already seen you in your most intimate aspect."[89] Thus this case involved a gross invasion of privacy in the ordinary sense of that word as well as in the constitutional-law sense.

I have already referred to various opinions in *Bowers* to illustrate several issues of constitutional interpretation: the emphasis in Black-mun's dissent on the affirmative conception of privacy as individual liberty and autonomy, following in the spirit of Douglas's concurrence in *Roe;* White's position that the Court's protection of privacy usurps the legislative function; and White's gross understatement of what is at stake, from the individual's perspective, in the privacy cases. Here I will focus on the larger interpretive issue of which Justice White's (mis)characterization of what is at stake is a facet: the level of concreteness or generality that should be used in constitutional interpretation. I have already explored another aspect of this broader issue, in terms of partic-ular constitutional provisions, in my discussion of the debate between Harlan and Black (as well as between Harlan and Stewart) in *Griswold:* whether one can extrapolate a general right of privacy from particular constitutional provisions protecting specific forms of privacy.

Concreteness vs. Generality

At every possible juncture, White's majority opinion in *Bowers* took the narrowest possible view and Blackmun's dissent took a starkly contrasting view. I will describe five facets of White's overly literal, a-contextual approach. First, as already noted, White persisted in inaccurately describing the nature of the asserted right as the relatively narrow (and relatively controversial) one of engaging in homosexual sodomy, despite the broader scope of the Georgia statute, of the plaintiffs' pleadings and briefs, and of the relevant precedents. He stated: "The issue presented is whether the Federal Constitution confers a fundamental right upon homosexuals to engage in sodomy. . . ."[90] This insistently narrowed focus was described by Justice Blackmun as "the Court's almost obsessive focus on homosexual activity."[91]

In contrast with White's artificially concrete and literalistic approach to the case, Justice Blackmun's dissent provided the following description of what was really at stake:

> This case is no more about "a fundamental right to engage in homosexual sodomy," as the Court purports to declare, . . . than *Stanley* v. *Georgia* . . . was about a fundamental right to watch obscene movies, or *Katz* v. *United States* . . . was about a fundamental right to place interstate bets from a telephone booth. Rather, this case is about "the most comprehensive of rights and the right most valued by civilized men," namely, "the right to be let alone."[92]

The second manifestation of White's overly concrete interpretive approach in *Bowers* was his treatment of the constitutional privacy precedents. Just as White misstated the issue presented in *Bowers* itself, he likewise misstated the Court's past privacy decisions by concentrating very narrowly on the particular facts they involved and refusing to extrapolate beyond them. He described *Pierce* v. *Society of Sisters*[93] and *Meyer* v. *Nebraska*[94] as involving "child rearing and education," *Prince* v. *Massachusetts*[95] as involving "family relationships," *Skinner* v. *Oklahoma*[96] as involving "procreation," *Loving* v. *Virginia*[97] as involving marriage, and *Griswold, Eisenstadt* v. *Baird,*[98] and *Roe* as involving the decision "whether or not to beget or bear a child."[99] Given this narrow, concrete focus on the specific facts involved in each case, it is not surprising that White stressed the particular facts presented in *Bowers* —which were, clearly, different from the particular facts involved in the earlier cases—and therefore concluded that it involved constitutionally distinguishable issues:

[N]one of the rights announced in these cases bears any resem-
blance to the claimed constitutional right of homosexuals to engage
in acts of sodomy. . . . [N]o connection between family, marriage,
or procreation on the one hand and homosexual activity on the
other has been demonstrated.[100]

Justice Blackmun effectively countered Justice White's unduly literal and fact-bound reading of the earlier cases and noted that it
ignored the broader underlying purposes reflected in the Court's
specific rulings:

We protect those rights not because they contribute . . . to the
general public welfare, but because they form so central a part of
an individual's life. . . . "[T]he concept of privacy embodies the
'moral fact that a person belongs to himself and not others nor to
society as a whole'". . . . And so we protect the decision whether
to marry precisely because marriage "is an association that promotes
a way of life; a harmony in living . . . ; a bilateral loyalty. . . ." . . .
We protect the decision whether to have a child because parenthood
alters so dramatically an individual's self-definition. . . . And we
protect the family because it contributes so powerfully to the happiness of individuals, not because of a preference for stereotypical
households. . . .
      The fact that individuals define themselves in a significant way
through their intimate sexual relationships with others suggests, in
a Nation as diverse as ours, that there may be many "right" ways
of conducting those relationships, and that much of the richness
of a relationship will come from the freedom an individual has to
choose the form and nature of these intensely personal bonds.[101]

The contrasts between White's literalistic, concrete approach and
Blackmun's more abstract approach are highlighted in their differing
interpretations of one particular precedent: *Stanley v. Georgia.*[102] *Stanley,* which Blackmun described as a "pivotal" precedent, invalidated a
statute that criminalized the private possession of obscene material in
one's home, despite the fact that such material could constitutionally
be prohibited in public places. In *Bowers,* the plaintiff and the dissent
relied on *Stanley*'s broad language about the sanctuary of the home in
support of the claimed right of intimate sexual relations in this setting.
In contrast, in an effort to limit *Stanley*'s precedential force for *Bowers,*

White's majority opinion focused on the fact that *Stanley* involved printed materials, and therefore concluded that "the decision was firmly grounded in the First Amendment."[103] However, as Blackmun's *Bowers* dissent pointed out, *Stanley* itself described the issues presented in appropriately broad and abstract terms.[104] Let's let the *Stanley* opinion speak for itself as to the right it upheld: "[A]ppellant is asserting . . . the right to satisfy his intellectual and emotional needs in the privacy of his own home."[105] Accordingly, consistent with *Stanley*'s actual holding, Blackmun's dissent in *Bowers* concluded:

> The right of an individual to conduct intimate relationships in the intimacy of his or her own home seems to me to be the heart of the Constitution's protection of privacy.[106]

A fourth facet of the majority's unduly cramped approach to constitutional interpretation was its skewed version of the relevant legal history. The majority's "almost obsessive focus"—to use Blackmun's term—on homosexual sodomy distorted its perspective on the history of the legal treatment of sodomy. The majority zeroed in on past prohibitions on homosexual sodomy, ignoring the fact that the vast majority occurred in tandem with prohibitions on heterosexual sodomy as well. Therefore, the Court's conclusion that there is a tradition of banning *homosexual* sodomy is actually incorrect, as Justice Stevens's dissent explained.[107]

Finally, the majority's characterization of the adverse precedential effect of its ruling is as narrowly concrete, and hence as inaccurate, as the other aspects of its opinion. Blackmun's dissent pointed out this flaw:

> The Court claims that its decision today merely refuses to recognize a fundamental right to engage in homosexual sodomy; what the Court really has refused to recognize is the fundamental interest all individuals have in controlling the nature of their intimate associations with others.[108]

Harvard Law professor Laurence Tribe, who argued *Bowers* in the Supreme Court for the American Civil Liberties Union, forcefully explained why the *Bowers* majority's consistently concrete approach to constitutional interpretation is antithetical to the purpose of fundamental rights analysis, especially when the rights of a despised minority are at issue:

> When the Court uses the history of violent disapproval of the behavior that forms part of the very definition of homosexuality as the basis for denying homosexuals' claim to protection, it effectively inverts the equal protection axiom of heightened judicial solicitude for despised groups and their characteristic activities and uses that inverted principle to bootstrap antipathy toward homosexuality into a tautological rationale for continuing to criminalize homosexuality. Therefore, *in asking whether an alleged right forms part of a traditional liberty, it is crucial to define the liberty at a high enough level of generality to permit unconventional variants to claim protection along with mainstream versions of protected conduct.*[109]

A Substantive Constitutional Shift

In addition to the issue of the level of abstraction or generality at which interpretation occurs, *Bowers* also well illustrates another common issue of constitutional interpretation in privacy cases: it shows that what is at stake, ultimately, is a substantive philosophical difference. Differing approaches to interpretation simply reflect that substantive difference. This is certainly true for varying views as to which party has the burden of proof and how heavy it is.

Professor Anne Goldstein explored this theme in a 1988 article about *Bowers* in the *Yale Law Journal.*[110] As she explained, the *Bowers* majority reflected the classic conservative or statist philosophy. It accepted Georgia's argument that even irrational popular prejudices should be enforced to preserve the very existence of society.[111] In contrast, Blackmun's dissent reflected the classic liberal or libertarian philosophy. It suggested that one's right to behave as he or she chooses may be limited only to prevent harm to oneself or to others.[112] Thus *Bowers* was a significant victory for substantive conservative values, as well as for the conservative approach to constitutional interpretation. According to Professor Goldstein, *Bowers* apparently shifted the argument about whether an activity is protected by the constitutional right of privacy away from the liberal paradigm, which had prevailed in *Griswold* and *Roe*. Under that approach, individual liberty is protected unless it sufficiently endangers society. *Bowers* moved the analysis of privacy claims to the conservative paradigm, under which state restrictions are upheld so long as they are sufficiently consistent with "traditional values."[113]

Professor Goldstein's understanding of *Bowers* is consistent with the Court's citation of it in *Barnes* v. *Glen Theatre,*[114] in which five justices held that an Indiana statute prohibiting public nudity could be applied to nude barroom dancing, consistent with the First Amendment, even though the dancing was viewed only by admission-paying adults and there was no evidence that it caused or threatened any harm, such as illegal or violent conduct. The justices who agreed on this result arrived at it through three separate rationales. Four of them expressly ruled that nude barroom dancing is a form of expression, conveying messages of eroticism and sensuality, that is within the scope of the First Amendment.[115] Nevertheless, four justices ruled that this expression could still be banned merely because the majority of the community presumably found it morally offensive.[116] In attempting to justify this imposition of majoritarian value judgments upon dissenting or unpopular minorities, thereby depriving the latter of constitutional rights, two of the opinions expressly relied upon *Bowers*.

Barnes took a significant further step in the *Bowers* direction of weakening individual rights. In *Bowers,* the Court refused to recognize what it considered to be a new implied fundamental right, and therefore subjected the Georgia statute at issue only to "rational basis" review. The Court then ruled that "the presumed belief of a majority of the electorate in Georgia that homosexual sodomy is immoral and unacceptable" constituted such a rational basis, sufficient to survive this low level of constitutional scrutiny.[117] In support of that conclusion, the Court said, "The law . . . is constantly based on notions of morality, and if all laws representing essentially moral choices are to be invalidated under the Due Process Clause, the courts will be very busy indeed."[118] But the *Barnes* plurality quoted the foregoing passage in an attempt to justify a more sweeping holding—namely, that restrictions upon the expressly protected and traditionally "preferred" constitutional right of free speech could be justified on the basis of the community's presumed sense of morality. The departure that this represented from the Court's past rulings regarding constitutional rights is underscored by the following cautionary note in Justice Harlan's opinion in *Poe* v. *Ullman:*

Where . . . we are dealing with . . . "a basic liberty," . . . "there are limits to the extent to which the presumption of constitutionality can be pressed," . . . and the mere assertion that the action of the State finds justification in the controversial realm of morals cannot justify alone any and every restriction it imposes.[119]

Justice Antonin Scalia's concurring opinion in *Barnes* also relied on *Bowers* to support his express rejection of what Professor Goldstein labeled "the liberal paradigm." He wrote as follows:

The dissent confidently asserts . . . that the purpose of restricting nudity in public places in general is to protect nonconsenting parties from offense; and argues that since only consenting, admission-paying patrons see respondents dance, that purpose cannot apply. . . . Perhaps the dissenters believe that "offense to others" *ought* to be the only reason for restricting nudity in public places generally, but there is no basis for thinking that our society has ever shared that Thoreauvian "you-may-do-what-you-like-so-long-as-it-does-not-injure-someone-else" beau ideal—much less for thinking that it was written into the Constitution. . . . Our society prohibits, and all human societies have prohibited, certain activities not because they harm others but because they are considered . . . immoral.[120]

The clash of both interpretive perspectives and substantive values in the *Bowers/Barnes* majority and dissents was aptly capsuled by Professor Tribe in the following observation: "The relevant question is not what Michael Hardwick was doing in the privacy of his own bedroom, but what the State of Georgia was doing there."[121] Unfortunately, the Court's majority viewed the issue from the opposite perspective.

'THE RIGHT TO BE LET ALONE'

A fitting conclusion for my discussion of these three major constitutional privacy cases is what I regard as the most eloquent statement of the broad scope of constitutional privacy or autonomy, which justifies interpretive approaches designed to maximize that fundamental right. This statement, from a seminal Supreme Court dissent, was cited, and portions of it were quoted, in many opinions in this more recent privacy trilogy, including those that espoused appropriately expansive interpretive approaches.[122] I am referring to Justice Brandeis's famous dissent in *Olmstead* v. *United States.*[123] Since *Olmstead* was reversed in *Katz* v. *United States,*[124] Justice Brandeis's earlier dissent now enunciates accepted constitutional wisdom.

This often cited opinion serves to reorient us, away from the crabbed, concrete, literalistic approach of Justice White in *Bowers,* and toward the more expansive approach best exemplified more recently by Justice Harlan in *Griswold* and *Poe,* Justice Douglas in *Roe,* and Justice Blackmun in *Bowers.* According to Justice Brandeis, this is what is at stake in terms of constitutional privacy:

> "We must never forget," said Mr. Chief Justice Marshall in *McCul-loch* v. *Maryland,* "that it is a Constitution we are expounding." . . . Clauses guaranteeing to the individual protection against specific abuses of power must have a . . . capacity of adaptation to a changing world. . . .
>
> Time and again, this Court in giving effect to the principle underlying the Fourth Amendment, has refused to place an unduly literal construction upon it. . . . The narrow language of the Amendment has been consistently construed in the light of its object.
>
> The protection guaranteed by the Amendments is much broader in scope [than their literal language]. The makers of our Constitution undertook to secure conditions favorable to the pursuit of happiness. They recognized the significance of man's spiritual nature, of his feelings and of his intellect. They knew that only a part of the pain, pleasure and satisfactions of life are to be found in material things. They sought to protect Americans in their beliefs, their thoughts, their emotions and their sensations. They conferred, as against the Government, the right to be let alone — the most comprehensive of rights and the right most valued by civilized men. To protect that right, every unjustifiable intrusion by the government upon the privacy of the individual, whatever the means employed, must be deemed a violation.[125]

6

Shall We Ratify the New Constitution? The Judicial Manifesto in *Casey* and *Lee*

Handed down on the last day of the term, *Planned Parenthood* v. *Casey*[1] punctuated the Supreme Court's 1991-92 labors with an outsized exclamation point. Expectations could not have been higher. The votes to overturn *Roe* v. *Wade,* pro-lifers hoped and pro-choicers feared, were there. All charted courses for a post-*Roe* world.

The unexpected outcome was doubly significant: *Casey* (and Clinton's election) secured *Roe* for the next generation, and the distribution of votes in *Casey* revealed judicial commitments likely to be just as long-lived. Justice Clarence Thomas, to the surprise of few, joined Chief Justice William H. Rehnquist and Justices Byron R. White and Antonin Scalia on the right, and Justices John Paul Stevens and Harry A. Blackmun took their accustomed places on the left. The critical development was the emergence of what commentators immediately christened the "moderate center," composed of Justices David H. Souter, Sandra Day O'Connor, and Anthony M. Kennedy.

Gerard V. Bradley is a professor of law at Notre Dame Law School. He is the author of, among other works, *Church-State Relationships in America* (Greenwood Press, 1987), which is an extended historical argument in favor of a non-preferentialist interpretation of the Establishment Clause.

Kennedy's vote was the most unexpected, fairly construed as a conversion experience. He had joined Rehnquist's opinion in *Webster* v. *Reproductive Health Services* (1989), which the Chief Justice essentially reproduced as a partial dissent in *Casey*. Kennedy's *Casey* vote rankled the more because of rumors that he changed sides late in the term at the urging of either (depending on which rumor you heard) Professor Laurence Tribe or Justice Blackmun.

There is good reason to think that the *Casey* groupings are not casual dalliances. The desperately high political stakes clearly prompted, at least for the swing-voting centrists, an extraordinary period of reflection and contemplation, almost a dark night of the judicial soul. By the standards of the genre, their plurality opinion is an epic, a signature piece. It is a primer on the nature of our polity, the Court's pivotal role in it, and constitutional adjudication. *Casey* looks like a road map to the future of our constitutional law.

There is another good reason to think the *Casey* groupings are serious commitments: they reproduce the pattern of another of the term's great decisions, *Lee* v. *Weisman*,[2] which invalidated a middle school graduation prayer. Decided on the Wednesday before *Casey's* Monday announcement, *Lee* reconfirmed the Court's commitment to the privatization of religion. That project crested in 1985, and there had been reason to think it would recede, even disappear. The tide has apparently rolled back in.

Lee's deepest importance is visible only in the light shed on it by *Casey*. If *Casey* is the exclamation point, *Lee* is the proximate semicolon. The two cases emerged from the same judicial soul-searching and should, I submit, be seen as two chapters of one judicial manifesto. I shall argue that this profound, two-part statement cannot reasonably be construed as an interpretation of the 1787 Constitution as amended. It is really the summation of a comprehensive judicial project, dating almost entirely from World War II and mostly from 1960. Recent judicial statements, not the Constitution, are its authoritative supports. The decisions are justified by the rational appeal of a theory of the human person and a normative view of the judicial function in a pluralistic democracy.

But not quite entirely. The justices do not, indeed, offer *Casey, Lee,* and the judicial project they consummate as interpretations of settled authority (the Constitution). They are offered as enactments in search of authority. The authority sought, they further indicate, is ratification by the people.

I call this judicial construction the New Constitution. It is being offered to us for ratification. Should we ratify it?

CASEY, LEE, AND THE MEGARIGHT

In *Planned Parenthood* v. *Casey,* the Court, while reaffirming the holding in *Roe* v. *Wade* that abortion was a fundamental constitutional right, modified the standard for review of government regulations regarding that right. Discarding the trimester framework that *Roe* had created, the Court substituted a standard that would invalidate state regulation of abortion before viability only if it created "an undue burden" on the right of abortion. Under that standard, the Court upheld the requirement in a Pennsylvania statute that women seeking an abortion wait for twenty-four hours and be informed of the nature of the procedure, the health risks of abortion and of childbirth, and the gestational age of the fetus. It also upheld a requirement that a minor obtain the consent of a parent or guardian before having an abortion. The Court struck down, however, a spousal notification requirement.

The Establishment Clause was at issue in *Lee* v. *Weisman.* As was customary, Robert E. Lee, a middle school principal in Providence, R.I., invited a clergy member to deliver an invocation and benediction at the school's graduation ceremony in June 1989. As was also customary in Providence public schools, the principal told the clergyman, Rabbi Leslie Gutterman, that the prayers should be non-sectarian and gave him a pamphlet reiterating that advice, as well as advising that the prayer be composed with "inclusiveness and sensitivity." Four days before the ceremony, Daniel Weisman, whose daughter Deborah was in the graduating class, sought in her behalf in federal district court a temporary restraining order to prevent school officials from including a prayer in the graduation ceremony. The motion was denied, but in July Weisman sought a permanent injunction against the inclusion of prayers in Providence's middle and high school graduation ceremonies. The district court held that such prayers were unconstitutional, and the U.S. Court of Appeals for the First Circuit affirmed the holding. Daniel Weisman subsequently prevailed in the Supreme Court by a 5-to-4 vote.

Besides their temporal proximity, *Casey* and *Lee* possess these suggestive commonalities. Both were decided by the same five-member majority, with Thomas joining Scalia, Rehnquist, and White in dissent. David Souter threw himself a coming-out party in both *Lee* and *Casey.* Earlier, his views on both church-state and *Roe* had been unclear. Now, writing a separate concurrence in *Lee,* Souter positioned himself somewhere between the "moderate" Kennedy and the (very) liberal Blackmun and Stevens, but not before rehashing the same bad history that had derailed Establishment Clause analysis in the seminal *Everson* v. *Board of Education* (1947).

Both *Lee* and *Casey* dashed reasonable hopes of cultural conservatives. The unsurpassed dasher of hopes in *Lee* was also Justice Kennedy, who wrote the majority opinion. In 1989, Kennedy's opinion in *Allegheny County* v. *ACLU,* handed down the same day as *Webster,* had set forth what entered church-state lore as "coercion" analysis. It portended the eviction from Establishment Clause jurisprudence of "no endorsement" analysis, the strict separationists' best friend.

Kennedy would deny that in *Lee* he deviated from his *Allegheny* analysis. If he did not, then he must not have meant in *Allegheny* what he seemed to mean. Kennedy's tolerance for "coercion," it seems after (but not before) *Lee,* borders on the fastidiously squeamish: "coercion" analysis is practically indistinguishable from the separationist alternatives of Blackmun, Stevens, and O'Connor that, it seemed, he rejected back in 1989. (Note: those three justices joined Kennedy's *Lee* opinion, though Blackmun also wrote separately.) "Coercion" in *Lee* was the "involuntary" presence of Deborah Weisman at a religious display by public authority. (Attendance was not mandatory, but the majority of justices treated it as virtually compulsory.) How is that distinguishable from the involuntary encounter of a great number of citizens, including children, with a nativity scene displayed at a county courthouse that these citizens must enter involuntarily, perhaps because of a subpoena? But Kennedy *upheld* such displays in 1989.

Applying the Megaright

So much for suggestive similarities. *Casey* and *Lee,* upon closer inspection, articulate the *same* fundamental right. They apply the *same* right to different subject matters. Since this right is a real blockbuster, I call it the Megaright, or MR.

Among Casey's notable accomplishments was that it located respectable lodgings for the abortion right, previously an itinerant entitlement squatting—in different cases and according to different justices—in the Ninth Amendment, in a general right of privacy, and in a shantytown illumined by "penumbras" of the Bill of Rights. Now "[t]he controlling word in the case before us [Casey] is 'liberty.'"[3] Abortion is comfortably at home in the Due Process Clause of the Fourteenth Amendment.[4] Casey therefore not only perpetuated Roe but secured Roe better constitutional accommodations than it had ever enjoyed before.

Some judicial high-stepping got things rolling. First, the Casey "centrists" disposed of the Constitution, a "literal reading" (their phrase) of which suggests a limitation of "process." But no amount of better "process" would change their opinion of the Pennsylvania abortion law. I call their argument here stare decisis (the practice of following prior judicial holdings) squared: the plurality relied upon Justice Brandeis's reliance upon precedent to overcome his (and their) reservations about "substantive due process." They announced themselves satisfied that through due process "all fundamental rights comprised within the term liberty are protected" against government invasion.[5]

Then, "[t]he most familiar [!] of the substantive liberties protected by the Fourteenth Amendment are those recognized by the Bill of Rights." But protected liberties "are not exhausted by the precise terms of the specific [Bill of Rights] guarantees."[6] Which "fundamental rights" escaped the Framers' notice when they put together the Bill of Rights? "[P]ersonal decisions relating to marriage, procreation, contraception, family relationships, child rearing, and education."[7] Authority? Judicial precedent, particularly the contraception cases of Griswold, Eisenstadt, and Casey.

The Casey joint-opinion writers recognized, as did the Roe majority, that abortion is a very different question from contraception. What the Court had needed all along, in fact, but had yet to produce in a form acceptable to a majority, was a principle capable of embracing abortion and contraception (and marriage, procreation, child-rearing, and the like). Casey supplied it. "These matters, involving the most intimate and personal choices a person may make in a lifetime, choices central to personal dignity and autonomy, are central to the liberty protected by the Fourteenth Amendment."[8]

May public authority assist us in making worthy decisions about these matters? No. "At the heart of liberty is the right to define one's own concept of existence, of meaning, the universe, and of the mystery of human life. Beliefs about these matters could not define the attributes of personhood were they formed under the compulsion of the State."[9]

The Unencumbered "Person"

In the Mystery Passage above, the *Casey* plurality deployed a theory of "personhood" to rationalize the disparate rights protected by substantive due process, including abortion. Again, precedent was decisive. That is, the Court could have concluded that some of the rights previously recognized in judicial decisions were unfounded, and rationalized the remainder as (traditional) family privacy cases. The Court did not. Instead, having used the liberty clause as a ladder to ascend to the mountaintop, the Court could now kick it away: the word "person" appears repeatedly in the Constitution (denoting, as Blackmun insisted in *Roe,* only "postnatal human beings"). It doesn't matter anyway. One can readily grant apart from the authority of the Constitution that government ought to treat persons as "persons," with all that the word implies. The disagreement is over *what* it implies, and what institutional arrangements—judicial review or legislative or executive protection or some complex division of final authority among the three, and between the states and the federal government—best secure the attributes of personhood to persons. Authority (e.g., the Constitution) is usually the way a politically organized people settles such important matters.

What of *Lee?* Its subject matter, unlike that of *Casey,* was not controversial: the Bill of Rights *does* mention religion. (Does it matter? Is not religious liberty an attribute of "personhood"?) What *is* controversial in *Lee?* Specifying "coercion," "conformance," compulsion, to ensure that Deborah Weisman's religion is truly hers, that her faith is not imposed by the state. *Lee* v. *Weisman*'s "coercion" talk is an exquisitely refined analysis of *Casey*'s "person[hood]": a being defined by hyper-voluntary choice *(Lee)* about deep, personal decisions *(Casey)*.

Wary of transporting *Lee*'s coercion analysis to moral questions like those in *Casey?* Well, the Mystery Passage ("At the heart of liberty is the right to define one's own concept of . . . the mystery of human life") is about as good a definition of what the Court means by religion (as in, "freedom of . . .") as you will find. And there is in the *Lee* opinion absolutely no information about Deborah Weisman's religious commitments, if indeed she had any. For all we know, she believed everything the prayer-giving rabbi said. For all we know, she attended his temple. At a couple of points, Kennedy refers to Deborah as the "dissenter." At one point, he "assumes" that the prayers were offensive to her. But, clearly, Kennedy's term of choice for Deborah Weisman is "objector," and he so refers to her several times. The really telling passage is the one underwritten entirely by volition, pure and simple: "We turn our attention now to consider the position of the students, both those who desired the prayer and she who did not."[10] Kennedy did not ask about the "objector's" reasons for objecting, if indeed there were any.

We are talking in *Lee,* I submit, about the very same "person" we are talking about in *Casey:* the unencumbered, anterior-to-all-commitments (religious or otherwise), about-to-realize-her-humanity-not-by-choosing-wisely-but-simply-by-choosing "person." After all, there is room for only one theory of "personhood" in constitutional law. Constitutional law may be perverse, but it cannot be schizophrenic.

Still wary? Religious liberty has consorted with the morally autonomous self for a long time. *Casey* finally, and at a time when a breakup was reasonably expected, married them. Abortion must be freely available because, while not a solitary performance, "the abortion decision may originate within the zone of conscience and belief."[11] "The destiny of the woman must be shaped to a large extent on her own conception of her spiritual imperatives and her place in society."[12] So said the *Casey* plurality.

Casey-Lee perfects at least two decades of development in constitutional law during which civil liberties became the defining feature of that law. The Court has for that long been executing a pincers movement, surrounding the autonomous "person" with impregnable constitutional defenses. On the substantive-due-process flank, the justices were upgrading moral decisions (like contraception and abortion) to the practical status of "religion." On the religious flank, they were evacuating the definition of religion so that it met the new morality halfway. The justices have overseen the descent of religion from, in the 1950s, monotheism, to any belief in God[s], to "ultimate concern," all the way to where belief and disbelief are equally protected self-defining choices.

The crowning expression of this syncretism is *Casey*'s Mystery Passage. A propositional statement of it—a creed, really—is found in the law professors' pro-choice *Webster* brief:

The right of personal privacy stands against state domination over matters crucial to self-possession: self-definition in matters of value and conscience, and self-determination regarding ways and walks of life. By its force, government's hand is stayed from the diverse choices by which persons define their values, form and maintain communities of belief and practice, and bring up children whose lives in turn will be their own and not the State's. Accordingly, the Court's privacy doctrine has placed decisions regarding procreation, parenthood, and family formation at the core of those from which a non-totalitarian government must ordinarily be excluded.[13]

Substitute "liberty" for "privacy," per *Casey,* and you have a current statement of the Megaright.

Institutionalizing the Megaright

The MR must be a valuable, fragile creature, because *Casey-Lee* promised the Court's sustained and kind attention to its nurture, care, and protection. Constitutional law, per *Casey,* is no less than a matter of striking "the balance" between "individual liberty" and "the demands of organized society."[14] The Court allows (through recurrent exercise and by promises in *Lee* and *Casey*) that this "balance" resists translation into rules or useful guides. *Lee:* "Our [Establishment Clause] jurisprudence . . . is of necessity one of line drawing, of determining at what point a dissenter's rights of religious freedom are infringed by the State."[15] *Casey* evinces a similar determination to sort out, on a case-by-case basis, whether abortion rights have been "unduly burdened" by public authority. What does *that* mean? It is, the joint opinion says, "a shorthand for the conclusion that state regulation has the purpose or effect of placing a substantial obstacle in the path of a woman seeking to abort a nonviable fetus."[16] What is a "substantial obstacle"? The answer to that question will be worked out case by case. We have here an almost unimaginable (self) grant of jurisdiction —the power to *settle,* finally, the law—that the grantor/grantee exercises according to no rule but the promptings of conscience. The Supreme Court as court of equity, writ as large as possible.

The Supreme Court, in this position, does not actually decide *everything.* Congress, for instance, is not slated for closure. But the Court *may* decide *anything,* and clearly claims jurisdiction to do so. The justices reserve plenary authority to decide who decides. In a 1985 speech, then Justice William J. Brennan expressed this conception of his and his brethren's position in the cockpit and at the controls of public life. Though false as the *historical* assertion it was intended to be—and dubious (as we shall soon see) as the claim about popular ratification it aspired to be—what he said was revealing. Brennan spoke of "the American habit, extraordinary to other democracies, of casting social, economic, philosophical and political questions in the form of law suits, in an attempt to secure ultimate resolution by the Supreme Court."[17] "Ultimate" means final. *Casey:* "The Court's interpretation of the Constitution calls the contending sides of a national controversy to end their national division by accepting a common mandate rooted in the Constitution."[18]

WHAT ABOUT THE OLD CONSTITUTION?

A pertinent question is whether, after *Casey* and *Lee,* we can still reasonably consider the Supreme Court's pronouncements as interpretations of the 1787 Constitution as amended. I think not.

For one thing, *Lee* and *Casey* are by judicial confession *false* constructions of the 1787 Constitution as amended. Certainly in *Casey* and arguably in *Lee,* a majority sustained an interpretation of that charter that a majority believed to be incorrect. How so? In each case one or more votes was decided by *stare decisis,* the judicial practice of following (mostly for reasons having to do with the nature of adjudication and judge-made law) prior holdings, including erroneous ones. No need to psychoanalyze Kennedy to support my argument about *Lee*. I cite instead Souter's guarded, but still arguably decisive, reluctance to disturb separationist precedents in favor of persuasive constructions more friendly to religion.

Casey leaves little doubt how a majority of the present Court would have decided *Roe* v. *Wade*. It is as obvious as it can be without an explicit admission that one (or more) of the plurality would have sided with the *Casey* dissenters but for *stare decisis*. (A passing note: the *Casey* dissent is infinitely preferable to the majority opinion, but it too is deeply flawed. All but Justice Scalia and possibly Justice Thomas recognize abortion as a due-process "liberty interest." This is, in my view, both unjustified and mischievous.)

The Long Arm of Incorporation

There are still deeper ways in which *Lee* and *Casey* are not founded upon the (old) Constitution or its tradition of interpretation. *Lee* is an Establishment Clause case, but it mistakenly construes that provision to require government neutrality between an entire assembly's theism and *one* person's unexamined "objection." The clause really mandates an equality among religions, not parity between belief and disbelief. And this extravagant neutrality is traceable no deeper into our history than to a 1947 Supreme Court holding,[19] while the Establishment Clause dates to 1791. *Lee* examined the actions of a municipality created by state law. The First Amendment (which contains the Establishment Clause) begins, "*Congress* shall make no law . . ." (my emphasis). What had Congress to do with the invitation to Rabbi Gutterman? Nothing. How, then, did the Establishment Clause, and the federal judiciary, get involved?

By a process known as "incorporation," which its judicial facilitators have described as simple "application" of the Bill of Rights to the states. Barely begun in the 1920s, this entirely *judicial* process (no ordinary citizen has ever voted for incorporation, as such) started in earnest after World War II, when the Religion Clauses were "incorporated." Basically, incorporation is a phenomenon of the 1960s. It so altered our scheme of government that it alone might well be considered a new Constitution.

The really interesting and mostly overlooked thing is that incorporation is not what its promoters say it is: the *extension* of existing (ascertainable, settled) law to a new class of regulated actors (i.e., the states). For one thing, virtually all the states had equivalent if not identical provisions in their own bills of rights before federal judicial "incorporation." That is not surprising, since the federal Bill of Rights is a collection of provisions culled from the state bills of rights, circa 1787. More important, rarely has the Court applied extant law in "incorporating" cases. In some instances (e.g., non-establishment, self-incrimination) the "incorporated" norm was *invented* by the Supreme Court precisely in the incorporating cases. In other instances (e.g., right to counsel) the "incorporated" norm had been invented by the Court in another case. And in still others there was no norm to be incorporated at all: in search and seizure, for example, the Supreme Court simply *extended* its existing jurisdiction to *make* a common law of search and seizure. Finally, we have seen (in *Casey*) how the Court's due-process jurisprudence has confessedly *added* fundamental rights to those invented under Bill of Rights pretenses. All things considered, "incorporation" is synonymous with and almost entirely reducible to federal judicial power to make law. Simply put, "incorporation" means jurisdiction.

Oftentimes the justices claim not to make law but to (humbly) implement the commands of the Constitution and its Framers (Madison and that lot). But it is no argument from authority of the Framers to suggest, as the Court frequently does, that the Framers' warrant reaches through the ages because our judges address problems that the Framers attempted to solve. This is *the* critical move both in the cases and in academic defenses of them. The commonly addressed problems include (especially in the church-state area) "intolerance," "divisiveness," and "freedom of conscience." Generally, the problem of the "individual" versus "organized society," as well as "majority interests" versus "minority rights," serves as a link through the ages. Thus the Court allows in its "mere implementer" rhetorical moods that it may (!) not be applying the resolution of these questions ratified by the Founders. But, the justices continue, it is enough authority that they address the same problems that the Founders did.

This will not do. As Oxford legal philosopher (and no political conservative) Joseph Raz writes, *any* useful account of authority must treat the authoritative norm as an exclusionary reason: that is, the norm proposed as solution (or specification) must exclude independent evaluation of the merits of the case, or it is no authority at all.[20] Raz uses this example: legislators and administrators work out volumes of tax regulations in their effort to produce a fair and just income tax. A court, purporting to resolve a taxpayer's suit under the regulations, ignores all the enactments in favor of its idea of a "fair and just tax." Is the court treating the prior enactment as authority? Is it producing an "interpretation" of the tax laws? Hardly. To put Raz's completely sound point another way: authority attaches to the answer, not the question.

The Supreme Court has treated the Constitution as our hypothetical judge treated the tax code: as delineating the boundaries of subject matters (religion, privacy) over which law-making authority has been invested in courts. Actually, the plural (subject "matters") may be gratuitous. There is *one* problem: the individual v. the demands of organized society. And this problem gives rise to an unlimited jurisdiction to make law.

The evidence supports this judgment: despite continued protests of fidelity (e.g., by Kennedy in *Lee*) to the task of merely doing the "calculus of the Constitution," the opinions really offer a free-standing political morality (theory of "personhood," if you prefer) and a theory of institutions. Authority for this construction is, by and large, recent judicial statements. (I say "statements," not "authority" or "precedent"; the justices indiscriminately cite plurality opinions, concurrences, and dissents as "authoritative," as if they were majority opinions.) There is, in other words, considerably better reason to construe our constitutional law as a free-standing construction by judges over the last generation or so than to regard it as an interpretation of the Constitution. And, we now shall see, the justices know it. That is why they are asking us to ratify their New Constitution.

Does the Court Bind Conscience?

The great challenge to freedom of conscience today facing us therefore is, not whether there is a constitutional right to ingest peyote or to sacrifice animals, but this question: Do pronouncements of the Supreme Court, especially with respect to religion and morals, impose the same obligation on conscience that just laws impose when lawfully promulgated?

The question is *morally* urgent. It is true that today most analyses of law deny that law as such binds conscience. Sophisticated positivists like Raz argue from assumptions, including the existence of objective moral norms, that appeal to natural lawyers and other friends of the common morality. Raz's arguments are formidable. But they are not the arguments commonly proposed by American legal academics, who presuppose that law is simply violence, domination, ideology.

Natural lawyers (like myself) suppose that public authorities can make morally binding *now* what was morally optional *before,* at least within that vast range of actions that are neither absolutely required nor prohibited by the moral law. Right now I am at liberty both morally and legally to spend the twenty dollars in my pocket (or the hundred dollars in the bank) on Christmas gifts for my kids. But if I were informed that according to a regularly enacted law I owe a hundred dollars in taxes, I would be both morally and legally obliged to cut back on the Christmas gifts, if necessary, to pay the tax. Law, in this limited but important sense, *is* master of our conscience.

The Court would be a demanding master. By evacuating religio-moral authority from the public square and by disparaging popular majorities as well as legislators generally, the justices are proclaiming themselves the *sole* source of *just* rules.

If two conditions are met. Russell Hittinger relates the Thomistic tradition's teachings on the matter:

> [A] law can be invalid [i.e., fail to bind conscience] for two reasons: first, because of morally perverse content, as when a law contradicts either natural or divine law; or second, because the human agent acts *ultra vires,* beyond the power of his office. In short, the substantive moral properties of a legal enactment is a different issue than the morality of jurisdictional authority.[21]

Ordinarily, prior authoritative enactment—in this case, the Constitution—settles the matter of jurisdiction. But at least in principle, morally legitimate authority can be acquired. The sheer fact of effectiveness—that a given body's pronouncement can and will be taken as authoritative—may be taken to engender obligation *if* in truth the authority secures and advances the common good. This practically collapses the second criterion Hittinger cites into the first. Does the New Constitution truly secure and advance the common good? Each person must answer that question by his or her own best lights, especially in the matter of abortion.

In this light, *Casey* is, on its own terms, a desperate gamble that could not possibly succeed. As the "centrists" interpreted the political environment, the Court could either (1) faithfully interpret the 1787 Constitution, and take a lot of heat from pro-choicers who would charge the Court with politicking, or (2) propose a New Constitution, embodying the abortion right, and make *it* (really, the MR) the basis of an appeal *for* authority, or "legitimacy" (the Court's term). The centrists grabbed the second option. But it provided no way out. The object of *Casey* was to make peace in the abortion war by supplanting individual, conscientious evaluations of abortion with an authoritative rule of law that had somehow swung free of personal "moral codes." But, as we have just seen, the authority of the *Casey* rule rests upon individual opinions about the justice of abortion and, more generally, about the Court's capacity to promote the common good.

SHALL WE RATIFY THE NEW CONSTITUTION?

The balance of which I speak is the balance struck by this country, having regard to what history teaches are the traditions from which it developed as well as the traditions from which it broke. That tradition is a living thing. A decision of this Court which radically departs from it could not long survive, while a decision which builds on what has survived is likely to be sound.[22]

So, *Casey.* Now Justice Brennan, in his 1985 speech:

When Justices interpret the Constitution they speak for their community, not for themselves alone. . . . the Justices must render constitutional interpretations that are received as legitimate. The source of legitimacy is, of course, a wellspring of controversy in legal and political circles.[23]

After rejecting the Framers' intentions and democratic theory as very important sources of legitimacy, Brennan turned to the subtitle of his speech, "Contemporary Ratification":

Successive generations of Americans have continued to respect these fundamental choices and adopt them as their own guide to evaluating quite different historical practices. Each generation has the choice to overrule or add to the fundamental principles enunciated by the Framers; the Constitution can be amended or it can be ignored. . . . the burden of judicial interpretation is to translate "the majestic generalities of the Bill of Rights, conceived as part of the pattern of liberal government in the eighteenth century, into concrete restraints on officials dealing with the problems of the twentieth century."

We current Justices read the Constitution in the only way that we can: as Twentieth Century Americans. . . . But the ultimate question must be, what do the words of the text mean in our time?[24]

Are these prefaces to interpretation or to enactment? If interpretation, what is being interpreted—the old document or some living tradition? If a living tradition, whose tradition? Who pronounces deviating interpretations dead (the *Casey* passage says a Court decision that "radically departs from [tradition] could not long survive")? If the statements are prefaces to enactment, who is doing the enacting? Or is the thing in question a proposal that needs to be authoritatively received? If so, who receives, or ratifies, it?

Hard to say. The passages are purposely obscure because in them the justices are walking a gossamer line. They cannot sensibly proclaim themselves sole constitution-makers. But they cannot yield very much to the people (and their representatives) without undermining their arguments for the primacy of the judiciary. One thing is clear: in some decisive way, these are confessions that the Framers are not enough, that constitutional law has *so* deviated from the Constitution that the glance back is insufficiently legitimating. Hence the glance outward, at us. Our assent legitimates their proposal. 1787-88, all over again.

The rhetoric of *Lee* and *Casey* is, in my view, to be construed as latter-day *Federalist Papers:* extended arguments (primarily moral) to persuade each of us—collectively, the American people—to ratify the New Constitution. Talk in those cases of forestalling sectarian bloodletting, holding at bay intolerant majorities, the rule of law, the vision thing, is all, I submit, intended to persuade us to ratify and thereby legitimate the New Constitution. Should we?

132 GERARD V. BRADLEY

Taking the Measure of the New Constitution

Here are some reasons, briefly stated, to decline to ratify. I do not include among them the falseness of *Lee* and *Casey* as interpretations of the 1787 Constitution. They *are* false interpretations, but that, now that we are clearheaded, is beside the point. We are asking about an original act of constitution-making, not interpretation of settled authorities.

1. *The New Constitution is a bad constitution because it dangerously concentrates power in the hands of an elite unaccountable to those they govern.* The New Constitution greatly diminishes federalism and seriously impairs the separation of powers. Both are institutional arrangements that the Founders (correctly) thought preserved liberty by diffusing power. By contrast, the federal judiciary was then generally regarded, especially by the anti-federalists whose demands resulted in the Bill of Rights, as a menace to liberty. That is partly why most Bill of Rights provisions (in the Fourth through the Eighth Amendment) are directed against potential *judicial*—not legislative or executive—abuses. This further evidences just how radically the New Constitution departs from the (old) Constitution.

My point is not that the New Constitution is irrational (much less unintelligible), or that no reasonable person could support it, but that its central, defining feature is immense judicial power. (The MR is a close second.) Any society adopting such a proposal is, I submit, living dangerously.

2. *The New Constitution is divisive, precisely because it is defined by a stance on one side of the fault line in our society.* The MR resolves all the issues contested in our culture war (suicide, gay rights, abortion, and the like) in favor of one side.

Ironically, the justices are selling irenicism. They *say* that our politics is unsuited to settling hot moral issues, and that our politics is not to be trusted with the care and protection of individual rights when religion and morality wander into the public square. They *say* that *they* prescind from settling questions about the meaning of life. They *say* that only their neutral (if not Olympian) pronouncements have the capacity to heal our divisions. To be sure, neither *Casey* nor *Lee* minted this (by now) standard divisiveness rhetoric. The specter of "sectarian animosity" has been with us at least as far back as *Everson*.

But until sometime in the sixties "divisiveness" expressed little more than fear of Catholic political power. As Justice Rutledge wrote, following the initial conference to consider *Everson,* "[W]e all know that this is really a fight by Catholic schools to secure this money from the public treasury. It is aggressive and on a wide scale."[25] Rutledge feared that "the worst thing that could happen to this country would be to throw its religious demands, *financially* speaking, into politics" (emphasis mine).[26] In other words, divisiveness then had nothing to with abortion and sexual morality, upon which the churches were united, but concerned (at most) distributive justice, (at least) pork barrel.

Into the early 1970s the background of church-state litigation was still public aid to parochial schools. Divisiveness rhetoric persisted, but it was rarely sanguinary. In my view, *Roe* v. *Wade* changed all that. The Court's legitimacy was so threatened by that unfortunate decision that since then the justices have waged a take-no-prisoners rhetorical counteroffensive.

By June 24, 1992, divisiveness rhetoric was unforgivably hysterical. To support a textual observation that "democracy" requires "dialogue and dissent," and that religion is all about "theological decrees beyond" all "human deliberation," Justice Blackmun dropped this footnote:

Sigmund Freud expressed it this way: "a religion, even if it calls itself the religion of love, must be hard and unloving to those who do not belong to it." S. Freud, Group Psychology and Analysis of the Ego 51 (1922). James Madison stated the theory even more strongly in his "Memorial and Remonstrance" against a bill providing tax funds to religious teachers: "It degrades from the equal rank of Citizens all those whose opinions in Religion do not bend to those of the Legislative authority. Distant as it may be, in its present form, from the Inquisition it differs from it only in degree. The one is the first step, the other the last in the career of intolerance." The complete Madison, at 303. Religion has not lost its power to engender divisiveness. "Of all the issues the ACLU takes on—reproductive rights, discrimination, jail and prison conditions, abuse of kids in the public schools, police brutality, to name a few —by far the most volatile issue is that of school prayer. Aside from our efforts to abolish the death penalty, it is the only issue that elicits death threats." Parish, Graduation Prayer Violates the Bill of Rights, 4 Utah Bar J. 19 (June/July 1991).[27]

Blackmun has good reason to deflect the search for causes of lethal divisiveness. He was the author of *Roe* v. *Wade*.

The judicial disinformation campaign cannot withstand the reality test. With its failure goes the central prop of the New Federalist: that only with the Court vindicating the MR can we live together. Not so. As Martin Marty observes in the second volume of his series on modern American religion:

> All of these [great many social and political conflicts] were based in religious beliefs or else included profound religious motivations. . . . [But] evoking surprise in this story is the virtual absence of dead bodies as a result of these intense conflicts. Americans take for granted that their own religious controversies should be verbal and bloodless, that it is too late in history for religious wars. Yet near the end of the twentieth century television daily and newsmagazines weekly depict ways in which religion is a key element in conflicts which take enormous tolls in lives and property. In Northern Ireland, Iran, Iraq, Indonesia, Israel, India, the murderous parties bear names like Catholic, Protestant, Shi'ite, Sunni, Jew, Sikh, Hindu, and more, and their conflicts issue in death. Not so in America. While telling the story of these two decades we shall be especially alert to finding reasons why interreligious conflict has taken a different character here.[28]

Marty offers a definitive count of deaths due to religious conflict between 1919 and 1941 (the period that included Al Smith, Father Coughlin, Prohibition, and the Depression): four.

Divisiveness rhetoric still bites—its judicial proponents. That is because the justices have become sectarians. The Court has adopted a comprehensive moral conception (a theory of personhood), and imposes it by force of law. This is part of the problem of divisiveness, not its solution. Besides, has anything more divided American society in the past forty years than *Roe* v. *Wade?*

Some apologists for the New Constitution may resist my characterization of it as a "comprehensive moral conception." The *Casey* plurality, for instance: "Our obligation is to define the liberty of all, not to mandate our own moral code."[29] Of course, the *Casey* plurality might not fully understand their own position, especially when they say on the same page that "liberty" is a function of "personhood." But giving the plurality the benefit of the doubt does not exculpate them from the divisiveness accusation. As the Brennan speech and the *Casey* joint opinion make clear, *each* generation must decide for *itself* upon *its* constitution. Leaving aside enormous definitional problems (each "generation"?—do my children and I get to live under different constitutions, and my mother under still a third?), unless there is unanimous ratification, some *majority* will impose an entire structure of government *and* a determining political morality (the MR) upon a minority. That megaproblem of dissent is *not* solvable by the New Constitution. It is *about* the New Constitution. Perhaps that is why the justices tend to be desperately dramatic in their rhetoric: they need to save us from things (e.g., "sectarian bloodshed") that *everyone* will agree need to be avoided at (virtually) *all* costs. Look out when anyone tries to sell you something with this line: Buy my tonic, or it's Armageddon; those are your only options.

In truth, our best hope for holding this society together is not judicial messianism but our amazingly resilient though so imperfect politics. The Court might have abetted social pacification by sticking to the interpretation of settled authority—the 1787 constitution. It did not. And, on the precise issue of how to foster religious tolerance, I cannot surpass Justice Scalia's puncturing of his brethren's pretensions, in his *Lee* v. *Weisman* dissent:

> The founders . . . knew that nothing, absolutely nothing, is so inclined to foster among religious believers of various faiths a toleration—no, an affection—for one another than voluntarily joining in prayer together, to the God whom they all worship and seek. Needless to say, no one should be compelled to do that, but it is a shame to deprive our public culture of the opportunity, and indeed the encouragement, for people to do it voluntarily. . . . To deprive our society of that important unifying mechanism, in order to spare the nonbeliever what seems to me the minimal inconvenience of standing or even sitting in respectful nonparticipation, is as senseless in policy as it is unsupported in law.[30]

3. *The New Constitution offers a vision of a "free society" that is chilling and dehumanizing.* This point, along with the next, is basically an

argument about justice (as opposed to jurisdiction). Here I consider the social (for lack of a better term) consequences of the MR—the defining *substantive* feature of the New Constitution.

The MR lost a skirmish a few years ago in the *Michael H.* case, a constitutional challenge to California law's provision that the husband of a child's mother is the child's father where the couple are still cohabiting. *Casey,* however, establishes that Justice Brennan's *Michael H.* vision of our society is supported by a present majority of the Court. That vision is implicit in the New Constitution because it is a corollary of the MR:

> We are not an assimilative, homogeneous society, but a facilitative, pluralistic one, in which we must be willing to abide someone else's unfamiliar or even repellent practice because the same tolerant impulse protects our own idiosyncrasies. Even if we can agree, therefore, that "family" and "parenthood" are part of the good life, it is absurd to assume that we can agree on the content of those terms and destructive to pretend that we do. In a community such as ours, "liberty" must include the freedom not to conform.[31]

How long before a 12-year-old decides that his conception of the family differs from his parents', and vindicates his conception in court? (The interesting question is whether Mrs. Clinton will be publicly advocating this position before the Court embraces it.) How long before Catholic Charities is obliged to place children for adoption with lesbian couples? (Who could argue with the apparent suitability of the couple—one will be an Episcopal bishop, the other a fighter pilot.)

All that public authority may do under the New Constitution is "facilitate" realization of our humanity, and its tools are essentially negative: abstain from indications of moral value. According to *Casey,* there is a zero-sum relation between legal regulation and that liberty of choice that constitutes "personhood." But if law destroys value by restricting or eliminating choice, then where law is, there is . . . no humanity? An attack upon humanity? If so, our vast sphere of public life is, necessarily, dehumanizing. Consider now the implication of *this* proposition for one's right to personal security. How, more exactly, can we think about crime control and the sentencing of criminals under the New Constitution?

Others have pointed out that contemporary liberals like Brennan cannot *punish* criminals because they have abandoned the moral framework in which punishment makes sense. But they cannot effectively warehouse or deter criminals either. Why not? If law eliminates choice, what does incarceration do? According to Brennan, incarceration saps a man of his dignity. Incarceration is (virtual) annihilation of the person. Brennan says, we must do everything possible to avoid wrongful conviction. But once we see incarceration as the terminal point in society's relation with an individual, we will (should) do everything possible to avoid convicting anyone at all. Incarceration is personicide, indistinguishable from capital punishment.

4. *The New Constitution promises a regime in which the struggle of individuals to attain virtue will be impeded.*

But isn't a regime supremely devoted to individual choice the best way, philosophically speaking, to organize our common life? Isn't *that* the pivotal question roused by the referendum on the New Constitution? Isn't a vote against ratification a vote against freedom?

To answer the last question first, and directly: No. The answer to the second question depends upon what, exactly, is meant by the first. Certainly one should oppose the moral subjectivism—the view that what is good and what is evil is a matter over which individuals enjoy sovereignty—entailed by the MR. But choice *is* valuable. More exactly, it is the precondition for realization in our lives of the goods attainable through human action. Still, a limitless variety of lifestyle options is hardly necessary to enjoy effective choice. Even within a robust conception of natural law, *pace* jurists who seem unable to speak the word "moral" without adding "strict" before and "code" after it, there are (virtually) limitless opportunities for choice. Natural law proposes to guide choice, not to eliminate it. Natural law empowers us to attain those goods that we intuitively value and at which we implicitly aim. So, choice is valuable, but not *the* value. Without guidance by objective moral norms, choice enables us to destroy our character, and to degrade our humanity. By radically contrasting law to the possibility of virtue, the New Constitution robs persons of that limited but essential support of wholesome laws.

In any event, *is* radically free individual choice *really* the overriding objective of common life governed by the New Constitution? There is good reason to think it is not. A glance at the literature usually cited by proponents of the MR reveals that for most "choosers," abortion, suicide, and many sexual relationships, for examples, are experienced as coerced. The "choosers" actually respond to predicaments in which they perceive no options. This literature also says that homosexuality is biologically based, and that other victimless immoralities (gambling, drugs) arguably within the MR are considered mental illnesses. And, try as the guardians of the MR might, it will be a long time before we really "choose" most of our family members.

It is, frankly, difficult to find forthright defenses of free choice among proponents of the MR. Even on the Supreme Court. Given its understanding of religion (non-rational, if not non-cognitive) and its sociology of knowledge (there are subliminal but profoundly formative influences all around us), it is hard to imagine a convincing, coherent account by the Court of just how individuals freely choose belief over disbelief, or one set of beliefs over another set.

Provisionally, we may question whether "personhood" is really the organizing philosophical construct. Does it not explain more of the pertinent data (chiefly, the judicial opinions) to suppose instead that undergirding the New Constitution is *identity,* fundamentally a psychological construct? Self-esteem, as I understand the relevant literature, is indispensable to a healthy, functioning identity. Basically, there are two ways of acquiring and maintaining self-esteem. One is to strive to live up to impersonal standards. To the extent that I do this, I experience an appropriate self-respect or self-esteem. To the extent that I fail, I experience guilt and shame, pick myself up, and try again. This would seem, broadly speaking, the way to self-esteem traditionally taken by believers in the God of Abraham, Isaac, and Jacob, the God of Moses, to whom God communicated his expectations of his people, and the God of Jesus, who said, "Be ye perfect as your heavenly Father is perfect." The other path to self-esteem is to *eliminate* impersonal standards. This path is quite likely the way of the New Constitution.

IS THERE A THIRD WAY?

Before deciding for or against ratification, we should consider the possibilities for constructive change *within* institutional channels provided by the New Constitution. What opportunities are there for, say, the traditionalists in the culture war to mitigate (eliminate? reverse?) the baneful effects of the MR that I have sketched? May we, in other words, accept the New Constitution, expecting to change it—just as many of the ratifiers of the (old) Constitution accepted *it?*

I think not. The cardinal feature of the New Constitution is the insulation of decision by public authority from the public. We are talking therefore primarily of opportunities to effect change through the courts. But transferring cultural issues (religion, family, sexual morality) to the courts skews the resolution of them. At its best, the adjudicatory setting can scarcely take adequate account of the important but diffuse right of all persons—the community—to a decent cultural environment, to a healthful "moral ecology." The injury to parents (and their children) of bad examples gone unpunished, and the lost educative effect wrought by legal recognition of true morals, pale against the dissenter's claims of rights.

That is with the adjudicatory setting at its best—hardly what we are dealing with today. As practiced by courts in the last several decades, the rights of the community are translated into "collective," "majority," "government," or "state" "interests." Only individuals possess rights.

It gets worse.

So far, the side representing the common morality is visible, even if its position is systematically discounted and a bit distorted. The next move in the New Constitutional jurisprudence is to join "majority" at the hip to "intolerance" and "prejudice." Thus fused, "majority-intolerance" fails to defeat claims of individual rights. Majorities are the enemy of rights, even indicators that a right of some individual is actually present. That is, one's right to be a "dissenter," "conscientious objector," or "non-conformist" is, just a bit loosely speaking, what the new order protects, and that status is defended by relation to some "consensus" or "majority" or "mainstream" viewpoint. As the rhetorical strategy has it, majorities care only about conformity. They are congenitally intolerant. The MR is basically the right *not* to conform. When majorities get excited, it is likely that they are trying to exact conformity. Therefore, the more one litigant speaks of the community's interests, the more likely it is that on the other side is some lonely dissenter being railroaded into conformity.

Justice Stevens has cobbled these observations together into a formal constitutional doctrine. He has made the Establishment Clause into a brief for the MR. In *Webster* v. *Reproductive Health Services,* for example, Stevens concluded that only theological dogma could support the view that life begins at conception, and in *Cruzan* v. *Director, Missouri Department of Health* he said that dogma necessarily underwrote resistance to the "right to die." This is philosophical nonsense; believers can and do oppose abortion and euthanasia on grounds based on reason, not revelation. It is also constitutional nonsense, a false interpretation of the Establishment Clause. But, for Stevens, efforts to restore elements of traditional morality to public life are by definition unconstitutional.

The ride gets still rougher. Almost all judicial invalidation of laws against homosexual sex describes the fatal defect something like this: "The fact that a majority of citizens finds certain behavior offensive, that it offends their sensibilities, is not a sufficient ground for them to impose their moral sentiments upon persons with different moral views." In that one sentence are probably packed all the deformities in modern thought about the nature of morality and its relationship to decisions by public authority. For example, the *fact* of majority disapproval is a red herring. Anyone who is not brain-dead can see that the "fact" of my belief is no reason for me to do anything in addition to or apart from the reasons why I hold the belief. The emotivism implicit in these characterizations signals either disingenuousness or amnesia—total loss of the possibility of objective moral norms. The dogmatist and emotivist labels may be all that Stevens et al. *can* see, once objective morality has been dismissed or forgotten.

7

Toward a Structural Approach to Constitutional Interpretation

MARY ANN GLENDON

The philosopher Ludwig Wittgenstein once said that sometimes "the aspects of things that are most important for us are hidden because of their simplicity and familiarity."[1] Often we need the help of an outsider to notice what is right before our eyes. In teaching a course called Introduction to American Law to foreign lawyers doing graduate work at Harvard Law School, I am always fascinated at the glimpses that can be obtained — through their eyes — of our own legal system.

In truth, though, the insights I get from my foreign students remind me less of the late Wittgenstein than of the scene from the film *Young Frankenstein* where Gene Wilder as Dr. Frankenstein has his first meeting with the hunchback Igor. As they are driving together out to the ancestral castle, the doctor, trying to be friendly, says to Igor, "Perhaps I could do something about your hump." Igor replies, "What hump?" That is, foreign students in American law schools seem less surprised at what is on full display than at what is missing.

Mary Ann Glendon is a professor of law at Harvard Law School. Among her more recent books are *Rights Talk: The Impoverishment of Political Discourse* (1991) and *A Nation Under Lawyers* (1994).

141

Nowhere is this more true than in constitutional law, where most courses begin, not with a general overview of the area, but rather with a single court decision, usually *Marbury v. Madison*.[2] Persons trained abroad can see why we proceed this way in areas built historically on judge-made law, but they are genuinely puzzled about why the typical constitutional-law course does not begin with a study of the text, structure, and design of the Constitution. They are even more puzzled by the scant attention that many professors pay to the Constitution as the course goes on, and by the apparent lack of even a minimal consensus on the techniques to be used for construing that document.

In this last respect, the situation in the United States presents an interesting contrast with that in continental Europe, where substantial consensus exists (across a wide political spectrum) on the outlines of a general approach to constitutional interpretation.[3] That approach essentially consists of adapting to constitutional interpretation the traditional set of techniques that lawyers in civil-law systems had developed for dealing with their civil codes—the source of law that long had the same centrality in their legal world that case law has had in ours.[4] Needless to say, consensus on an approach does not preclude vigorous controversies about how the approach is to be applied. It would be as though most American lawyers had agreed that in interpreting our constitution we ought to use the techniques we have traditionally brought to the common law.[5] Naturally, agreement of that sort would not tell you much about how particular disputes would be resolved.

What I want to suggest is that we Americans in practice, more often than not, *do* bring a common approach (or, more precisely, a common set of habits) to constitutional interpretation. I will advance that thesis first in a form that is perhaps too strong, and then in a milder form. The stronger proposition is that, in practice, our courts and commentators tend to approach the Constitution in the same awkward way that Anglo-American lawyers have always dealt with all other forms of enacted law, and that the disarray that has long characterized our efforts at statutory interpretation is mirrored in constitutional interpretation. The milder version of my argument is that historical happenstance—in the form of certain traditional professional strengths and weaknesses—has had a greater influence on constitutional interpretation, here and abroad, than is generally recognized.

These craft traditions are an important but neglected part of the explanation for the state of affairs that has led prominent constitutional scholars to concede that "our understanding of constitutional interpretation remains in a primitive state."[6] A full development of that proposition obviously would require more space than is available here. So I will confine myself to advancing four points designed, not to cover the subject, but to call attention to it. First, I will hazard a few observations about why the skills of American lawyers in dealing with enacted law never rose to quite the same level as our case-law methods. Then, I will explain why, in my view, our relative weakness in dealing with enacted law became a particular problem for us toward the end of the nineteenth century, with regard to both statutes and the Constitution. Third, I will briefly note how many notable lawyers of the 1930s called attention to this problem and were ignored. Finally, I will offer a few comments on the current status of enacted law in the legal academy.

Our "Fear of Statutes"

Long ago Roscoe Pound observed:

[T]he common law has never been at its best in administering justice from written texts. It has an excellent technique of finding the grounds of decision of particular cases in reported decisions of other cases in the past. It has always, in comparison with the civil law, been awkward and none too effective in deciding on the basis of legislative texts.[7]

As Max Weber pointed out in his sociology of law, different legal systems had historically fostered the development of quite different arrays of professional skills.[8] Pound correctly observed in the 1930s that attitudes and practices formed by such "long-taught traditions" would not easily give way. Even today, lawyers trained in the Romano-Germanic civil-law systems are significantly less adept than we are at dealing with case law,[9] but we Anglo-American lawyers are less skilled than they in drafting and dealing with enacted law—be it regulations, statutes, codes, or constitutions. Karl Llewellyn, the chief draftsman of the Uniform Commercial Code, once noted the "unevenness, the jerkiness" of American work with statutes as contrasted with our work with case law.[10] Comparing us unfavorably in this respect to our civil-law counterparts, he wrote: "It is indeed both sobering and saddening to match our boisterous ways with a statutory text against the watchmaker's delicacy and care of a . . . continental legal crafts-man, or even of a good American lawyer when the language he is operating with is that not of a statute but of a document."[11] Anyone who talks to appellate judges often hears comment on the relative awkwardness of lawyers confronted with statutory questions.

The reason, as Weber indicated, lies in tradition. Historically it was judges and practitioners who took the lead in developing English law, while the civil law was developed primarily by university scholars, and was rationalized and systematized at a crucial stage by legislative codi-fications.[12] One might say that Anglo-American lawyers and Conti-nental lawyers are like athletes who, as a result of playing different sports, have developed muscular strength in different parts of their bodies. For centuries, as long as we worked sitting at the common-law bench, we didn't notice our spindly statutory legs. We had a simple set of tools that were adequate for dealing with pre-modern English statutes—statutes that typically did not purport, as European codes did, to be complete new sets of authoritative starting points for legal reasoning.[13] English judges, traditionally, treated statutes as a kind of overlay against the background of the common law, and tried where possible to construe them so as to blend them into the case law.

When the Trouble Started

Those crude techniques worked well enough until the late nineteenth century, when the bench was pulled out from under us by legislatures that began producing a new type of statute. It is somewhat startling for us to read today Roscoe Pound's statement that, before the Civil War, a lawyer could number on his fingers the statutes with an enduring effect on private law.[14] There was not only *more* legislation in the latter part of the century, but legislation of the type we would now call regulatory—laws for a busy industrial society, statutes that did not fit well with the pre-industrial common law.[15] As suffrage was ever more broadly extended, lawmakers experimented with social legislation.[16] They addressed themselves to the hours and conditions of work of women, children, and laborers in certain industries, and to the attempts of workers to organize. In a now familiar fashion, those whose interests were adversely affected by decisions of the popular branches took their complaints to the courts, with the well-known result that the Supreme Court embarked on its first sustained adventure with judicial review—the power it had claimed in 1803 but had till then rarely exercised.[17]

The behavior of the courts in the *Lochner* era is commonly said to show the degree to which the judiciary was in the service of the economically dominant classes.[18] But part of that story, as I have suggested, had to do with the history of the legal profession. The fact is that when American judges entered the relatively uncharted areas of interpreting these new types of statutes and reviewing them for conformity to the Constitution, they did not know quite how to go about it. (Bear in mind that as late as 1875, nearly half of the Supreme Court's caseload was still pure common-law litigation, but by 1925 that proportion had dropped to 5 per cent.[19])

Now here is a key point: most judges during those years of passage tended to proceed in the way they knew best. When they encountered gaps or ambiguities in the written law, their tendency was to fill them with the common law, rather than to search first for principles in the structure and design of the instrument. They fell back on their habitual practice of construing enacted law (including the Constitution) in such a way as to blend in with, rather than displace, the common-law background—a background where protection of property rights and freedom of contract were ensconced as leading principles. As Roscoe Pound put it, "[The common-law lawyer] thinks of the constitutional checks upon legislation as enacting common-law limitations, and systematically develops those checks in terms of the common law."[20]

Oliver Wendell Holmes and others, of course, insisted vigorously that the Constitution was not just an overlay on the private law of property and contract.[21] But that point seldom got across until the 1930s, and even then it was not fully absorbed.

Unheeded Warnings

An interesting question arose in the 1930s. Once it became clear that enacted law of various sorts had acquired a prominent and permanent place among the materials of legal reasoning, why did we not systematically attend to the study of legislative drafting, and to the development of more differentiated techniques for interpreting the new and more complex types of statutes? It is remarkable how many eminent legal figures in the 1930s and 1940s called attention to the urgent need to take up these matters in the nation's law schools. Cardozo's famous essay "A Ministry of Justice" led to the founding of the New York State Law Revision Commission (but to little else).[22] There were also classic pieces by Roscoe Pound, James M. Landis, Felix Frankfurter, and Karl Llewellyn.[23] Some of those lawyers, like Landis, had been architects of New Deal legislation; others, like Llewellyn, were leaders in the Uniform Law movement and the American Law Institute.

The cudgels were taken up again by Henry Hart and Albert Sacks, who wrote in the 1950s, "The hard truth of the matter is that American courts have no intelligible, generally accepted, and consistently applied theory of statutory interpretation."[24] And again by J. Willard Hurst in 1982: "Statute law is a pervasive element of twentieth-century legal order in the United States. . . . Yet the schools, the legal literature, and the legal profession have given remarkably little attention to the legislative process."[25] Yet, in the spring of 1992, a Harvard Law School curriculum committee reported that Harvard (like most other law schools) was still teaching the basic required first-year program "almost without regard to the coming of the regulatory state, and without recognition that statutes and regulations have become the predominant legal sources of our time."[26]

How do we explain the fact that, to this very day, American law schools have paid so little heed to calls from some of the century's leading legal thinkers to tool up for the tasks ahead? I do not have an answer, but I do have the uneasy feeling that something went wrong somewhere — as in that fateful scene where Dr. Frankenstein sends Igor to get a suitable brain for the man they are creating, and Igor accidentally grabs a jar from the shelf labeled "Beware! Abnormal Brain."

The Academy and Enacted Law Today

Whatever the reason, it was constitutional law, as we all know, and not legislation, that became the glamor subject. And the old, habitual practices continued to exert a strong influence on how courts and commentators dealt with the Constitution. The preference for judge-made over enacted law that had been so evident in the *Lochner* era enjoyed an Indian summer as the Court embarked on a second exciting adventure with judicial review. And that same reflexive preference persists today among many, perhaps most, teachers of constitutional law. They tend to treat the various provisions of the Constitution as mere starting points for free-wheeling judicial elaboration—as if that document had not established a regime that places important limits on both judicial and legislative law-making.

To take one recent example: the dust jacket of Laurence Tribe and Michael Dorf's 1991 book on constitutional interpretation summarizes their thesis as a proposal for construing the Constitution through techniques "that draw upon the traditions of the common law, whereby judges announce narrow rulings based on the reasoning of prior cases that conform to the central value or values in a specific constitutional clause."[27] At first, this sounds like a recommendation that common-law methods be adapted for constitutional interpretation. But what Tribe and Dorf actually prescribe is that constitutional rights should be articulated "at the highest possible level of generality."[28] To see that described as the method of the common law would come as quite a surprise to the generations of common-law lawyers who have strained to avoid high generalization, and who indeed have prided themselves on staying at the *lowest* level of generality that would get the job done. In fact, Tribe and Dorf's proposal is grounded neither in the common-law tradition nor in the structure of the Constitution.[29] It is just a new strategy for expanding selected rights, and a modern version of the old fear of enacted law, brought to a higher pitch by the likelihood that a new Court will trim back or discard some judge-made favorites.

Many years ago, it was an interesting theoretical question whether the institution of judicial review itself made it inevitable that the text and structure of the Constitution would be pushed into the background by case law. At a time when hardly any countries besides the United States had judicial review, Ernst Freund theorized that this was indeed a necessary consequence of giving such power to courts.[30] But now that systems of judicial review have been operating for several decades in other liberal democracies, we can see that the text need not be thrust so deeply into the background as it has been in the United States.[31] While recognizing that constitutions are more political and more open-ended than codes, Continental courts and scholars have found it natural to approach them by taking the text seriously, and proceeding from close textual analysis in the light of overall structure to consideration of purpose, both in the light of history and in the light of circumstances as they exist at the time of interpretation.[32]

Now, a polite but inquisitive person might say at this point: That is all very interesting, but would it make any difference as a practical matter if American courts and commentators approached the task of constitutional interpretation by attending more systematically to text and structure? The best responses to that question, I believe, are to be found in the work of a growing group of American legal scholars —Akhil Amar, John Hart Ely, Michael McConnell, and Geoffrey Miller, to name a few[33]—who are taking up the challenge of what the late Paul Bator called "constitutional architecture."[34] These scholars are exploring the relationship between our system of limited government and the system of rights that has been at the forefront of constitutional theory in recent years.[35] And they are approaching interpretive problems by attending to the overall design of the Constitution and the mutually conditioning relationships among its provisions. Without neglecting the rights tradition or the principles embodied in two centuries of precedent, they are attempting to restore separation of powers, federalism, and constitutional text and structure to "a central and appropriate place" in constitutional theory.[36]

As an example of the possible consequences of such a shift in judicial practices, consider the constitutionality of regulations that affect the enjoyment or use of property. Property, along with many other fine things, is certainly protected in the Constitution. But it is difficult to find warrant in text *or* precedential tradition for the *Lochner* Court's readiness to give property (and freedom of contract to acquire property) the same exalted position in constitutional law that it enjoyed in late-nineteenth-century common law. On the other hand, nearly to read property *out* of the Constitution, as the Court did later when it began to uphold regulatory legislation with little scrutiny of purposes or means,[37] seems indefensible for the same reason.

A holistic or structural approach would not produce "one right answer" to the so-called takings cases,[38] but it would tend to avoid those two extreme and atextual outcomes. And, on the positive side, it would tend to yield an array of plausible resolutions that would stand up in a more satisfactory way to the criteria by which common-law lawyers have traditionally judged their own work—treating like cases alike, assuring predictability and stability without foreclosing adaptation to changing social and economic circumstances.

That American courts or commentators will ever achieve consensus on this or any other approach seems highly doubtful. More probably, they will continue to lurch along from case to case and from theory to theory. As for the academy: it might be worthwhile to allocate more of our attention and energies to the long-neglected but important task of the study of legislation. For, if we are really interested in the democratic and participatory elements in our political tradition, practically everything remains to be done. And, who knows, attending to that area might have beneficial side-effects for constitutional interpretation.

At present, the legislator is the feared, mistrusted, and despised "monster" of American politics.[39] Many people, like the peasants with their pitchforks in the old version of *Frankenstein,* would like to render him powerless. More sophisticated burghers prefer just to ignore or avoid him.[40] But with help, and properly understood, he might turn out to have a "normal brain" after all, even to be the kind of guy you could invite to lunch—if you watched him carefully.

APPENDIX

Some Provisions of the Constitution of the United States

Following are the texts of "clauses" and other parts of the Constitution referred to in the essays in this book. The clauses are arranged alphabetically, after the Preamble. They are followed by Article III, Sections 1 and 2, dealing with the judicial power, and Amendments 1-15.

PREAMBLE: "We the People of the United States, in Order to form a more perfect Union, establish Justice, insure domestic Tranquility, provide for the common defence, promote the general Welfare, and secure the Blessings of Liberty to ourselves and our Posterity, do ordain and establish this Constitution for the United States of America."

Clauses

ATTAINDER CLAUSES (and ban on *ex post facto* laws): (1) "No Bill of Attainder or ex post facto Law shall be passed." *(From Article I, Section 9)* (2) "No State shall . . . pass any Bill of Attainder, ex post facto Law, or Law impairing the Obligation of Contracts[.] . . ." *(From Article I, Section 10)*

CITIZENSHIP CLAUSE: "All persons born or naturalized in the United States, and subject to the jurisdiction thereof, are citizens of the United

151

States and of the State wherein they reside." *(From Amendment 14, Section 1)*

COMMERCE CLAUSE: "The Congress shall have Power . . . [t]o regulate Commerce with foreign Nations, and among the several States, and with the Indian Tribes[.]" *(From Article I, Section 8)*

DUE PROCESS CLAUSES: (1) "No person shall be . . . deprived of life, liberty, or property, without due process of law[.]" *(From Amendment 5)* (2) "[N]or shall any State deprive any person of life, liberty, or property, without due process of law[.]" *(From Amendment 14, Section 1)*

ENUMERATION CLAUSE: "The enumeration in the Constitution, of certain rights, shall not be construed to deny or disparage others retained by the people." *(Amendment 9)*

EQUAL PROTECTION CLAUSE: "[N]or shall any State . . . deny to any person within its jurisdiction the equal protection of the laws." *(From Amendment 14, Section 1)*

ESTABLISHMENT AND FREE EXERCISE CLAUSE: "Congress shall make no law respecting an establishment of religion, or prohibiting the free exercise thereof[.]" *(From Amendment 1)*

GUARANTEE CLAUSE (also known as Republican Government Clause): "The United States shall guarantee to every State in this Union a Republican Form of Government[.] . . ." *(From Article IV, Section 4)*

NECESSARY AND PROPER CLAUSE: "The Congress shall have Power . . . [t]o make all Laws which shall be necessary and proper for carrying into Execution the foregoing Powers, and all other Powers vested by this Constitution in the Government of the United States, or in any Department or Officer thereof." *(From Article I, Section 8)*

PRIVILEGES AND IMMUNITIES CLAUSE: "The Citizens of each State shall be entitled to all Privileges and Immunities of Citizens in the several States." *(From Article IV, Section 2)*

PRIVILEGES OR IMMUNITIES CLAUSE: "No State shall make or enforce any law which shall abridge the privileges or immunities of citizens of the United States[.]" *(From Amendment 14, Section 1)*

SUPREMACY CLAUSE: "This Constitution, and the Laws of the United

States which shall be made in Pursuance thereof; and all Treaties made, or which shall be made, under the Authority of the United States, shall be the supreme Law of the Land; and the Judges in every State shall be bound thereby, any Thing in the Constitution or Laws of any State to the Contrary notwithstanding." *(From Article VI)*

TAKINGS CLAUSE: "[N]or shall private property be taken for public use, without just compensation." *(From Amendment 5)*

Article III

"SECTION 1. The judicial Power of the United States, shall be vested in one supreme Court, and in such inferior Courts as the Congress may from time to time ordain and establish. The Judges, both of the supreme and inferior Courts, shall hold their Offices during good Behavior, and shall, at stated Times, receive for their Services, a Compensation, which shall not be diminished during their Continuance in Office.

"SECTION 2. The judicial Power shall extend to all Cases, in Law and Equity, arising under this Constitution, the Laws of the United States, and Treaties made, or which shall be made, under their Authority;— to all Cases affecting Ambassadors, other public Ministers and Consuls;—to all Cases of admiralty and maritime Jurisdiction;—to Controversies to which the United States shall be a Party;—to Controversies between two or more States;—between a State and Citizens of another State;—between Citizens of different States;—between Citizens of the same State claiming Lands under Grants of different States, and between a State, or the Citizens thereof, and foreign States, Citizens or Subjects.

"In all Cases affecting Ambassadors, other public Ministers and Consuls, and those in which a State shall be a Party, the supreme Court shall have original Jurisdiction. In all the other Cases before mentioned, the supreme Court shall have appellate Jurisdiction, both as to Law and Fact, with such Exceptions, and under such Regulations as the Congress shall make.

"The trial of all Crimes, except in Cases of Impeachment, shall be by Jury; and such Trial shall be held in the State where the said Crimes shall have been committed; but when not committed within any State, the Trial shall be at such Place or Places as the Congress may by Law have directed."

(SECTION 3 *deals with treason.*)

Amendments 1-12

Amendments 1 through 10, the Bill of Rights, were ratified December 15, 1791.

AMENDMENT 1. "Congress shall make no law respecting an establishment of religion, or prohibiting the free exercise thereof; or abridging the freedom of speech, or of the press; or the right of the people peaceably to assemble, and to petition the Government for a redress of grievances."

AMENDMENT 2. "A well regulated Militia, being necessary to the security of a free State, the right of the people to keep and bear Arms, shall not be infringed."

AMENDMENT 3. "No Soldier shall, in time of peace be quartered in any house, without the consent of the Owner, nor in time of war, but in a manner to be prescribed by law."

AMENDMENT 4. "The right of the people to be secure in their persons, houses, papers, and effects, against unreasonable searches and seizures, shall not be violated, and no Warrants shall issue, but upon probable cause, supported by Oath or affirmation, and particularly describing the place to be searched, and the persons or things to be seized."

AMENDMENT 5. "No person shall be held to answer for a capital, or otherwise infamous crime, unless on a presentment or indictment of a Grand Jury, except in cases arising in the land or naval forces, or in the Militia, when in actual service in time of War or public danger; nor shall any person be subject for the same offense to be twice put in jeopardy of life or limb; nor shall be compelled in any criminal case to be a witness against himself, nor be deprived of life, liberty, or property, without due process of law; nor shall private property be taken for public use, without just compensation."

AMENDMENT 6. "In all criminal prosecutions, the accused shall enjoy the right to a speedy and public trial, by an impartial jury of the State and district wherein the crime shall have been committed, which district shall have been previously ascertained by law, and to be informed of the nature and cause of the accusation; to be confronted with the witnesses against him; to have compulsory process for obtaining witnesses in his favor, and to have the Assistance of Counsel for his defense."

AMENDMENT 7. "In suits at common law, where the value in controversy shall exceed twenty dollars, the right of trial by jury shall be preserved, and no fact tried by a jury, shall be otherwise reexamined in any Court of the United States, than according to the rules of the common law."

AMENDMENT 8. "Excessive bail shall not be required, nor excessive fines imposed, nor cruel and unusual punishments inflicted."

AMENDMENT 9. "The enumeration in the Constitution, of certain rights, shall not be construed to deny or disparage others retained by the people."

AMENDMENT 10. "The powers not delegated to the United States by the Constitution, nor prohibited by it to the States, are reserved to the States respectively, or to the people."

AMENDMENT 11. "The Judicial power of the United States shall not be construed to extend to any suit in law or equity, commenced or prosecuted against one of the United States by Citizens of another State, or by Citizens or Subjects of any Foreign State." *(Ratified February 7, 1795)*

(AMENDMENT 12 *establishes the electoral procedure for voting for President and Vice-President; ratified June 15, 1804.*)

Amendment 13

"SECTION 1. Neither slavery nor involuntary servitude, except as a punishment for crime whereof the party shall have been duly convicted, shall exist within the United States, or any place subject to their jurisdiction.

"SECTION 2. Congress shall have power to enforce this article by appropriate legislation." *(Ratified December 6, 1865)*

Amendment 14

"SECTION 1. All persons born or naturalized in the United States, and subject to the jurisdiction thereof, are citizens of the United States and of the State wherein they reside. No State shall make or enforce any law which shall abridge the privileges or immunities of citizens of the United States; nor shall any State deprive any person of life, liberty, or property, without due process of law; nor deny to any person within its jurisdiction the equal protection of the laws.

"SECTION 2. Representatives shall be apportioned among the several States according to their respective numbers, counting the whole number of persons in each State, excluding Indians not taxed. But when the right to vote at any election for the choice of electors for President and Vice-President of the United States, Representatives in Congress, the Executive and Judicial officers of a State, or the members of the Legislature thereof, is denied to any of the male inhabitants of such State, being twenty-one years of age, and citizens of the United States, or in any way abridged, except for participation in rebellion, or other crime, the basis of representation therein shall be reduced in the proportion which the number of such male citizens shall bear to the whole number of male citizens twenty-one years of age in such State.

"SECTION 3. No person shall be a Senator or Representative in Congress, or elector of President and Vice-President, or hold any office, civil or military, under the United States, or under any State, who, having previously taken an oath, as a member of Congress, or as an officer of the United States, or as a member of any State legislature, or as an executive or judicial officer of any State, to support the Constitution of the United States, shall have engaged in insurrection or rebellion against the same, or given aid or comfort to the enemies thereof. But Congress may by a vote of two-thirds of each House, remove such disability.

"SECTION 4. The validity of the public debt of the United States, authorized by law, including debts incurred for payment of pensions and bounties for services in suppressing insurrection or rebellion, shall not be questioned. But neither the United States nor any State shall assume or pay any debt or obligation incurred in aid of insurrection or rebellion against the United States, or any claim for the loss or emancipation of any slave; but all such debts, obligations and claims shall be held illegal and void.

"SECTION 5. The Congress shall have power to enforce, by appropriate legislation, the provisions of this article." *(Ratified July 9, 1868)*

Amendment 15

"SECTION 1. The right of citizens of the United States to vote shall not be denied or abridged by the United States or by any State on account of race, color, or previous condition of servitude—

"SECTION 2. The Congress shall have power to enforce this article by appropriate legislation." *(Ratified February 3, 1870)*

Notes

Chapter 1
WALTER BERNS

1. *Van Horne's Lessee* v. *Dorrance,* 2 Dallas 304 (1795), at 308–9.
2. *Ware* v. *Hylton,* 3 Dallas 199 (1796), at 211.
3. *Terminiello* v. *Chicago,* 337 U.S. 1 (1949), at 11.
4. *Hepburn* v. *Ellzey,* 2 Cranch 445 (1804), at 453.
5. *The Antelope,* 10 Wheat. 66 (1825), at 131.
6. *Ogden* v. *Saunders,* 12 Wheat. 213 (1827), at 346–47.
7. *Van Horne's Lessee,* at 310.
8. *Ogden* v. *Saunders,* at 347.
9. Robert Green McCloskey, ed., *The Works of James Wilson* (Cambridge: The Belknap Press of Harvard University Press, 1967), 1:329ff.
10. William Rawle, *A View of the Constitution of the United States,* 2d ed. 1829, in Philip B. Kurland and Ralph Lerner, *The Founders' Constitution* (Chicago and London: University of Chicago Press, 1987), 4:356ff.
11. James Madison to George Washington, Oct. 18, 1787, in Gaillard Hunt, ed., *The Writings of James Madison* (New York: G. P. Putnam's Sons, 1900-1910), 5:13–14.
12. Thomas Aquinas, *Summa Theologica,* I, q.95, a.1.
13. *Calder* v. *Bull,* 3 Dallas 386 (1798), at 398–99.
14. *Fletcher* v. *Peck,* 6 Cranch 87 (1890), at 143.
15. James Madison to Spencer Roane, Sept. 2, 1819, in Marvin Meyers, ed., *The Mind of the Founder: Sources of the Political Thought of James Madison,* rev. ed. (Hanover and London: Brandeis University Press, by University Press of New England, 1981), 361–62.
16. James Madison to Henry Lee, June 25, 1824, in Hunt, ed., *The Writings of James Madison,* 9:191; emphasis added. The passage quoted in the text begins as follows: "I entirely concur in the propriety of resorting to the sense in which the Constitution was accepted and ratified by the nation. In that sense alone it is the legitimate Constitution."
17. *Marbury* v. *Madison,* 1 Cranch 137 (1803), at 176, 178.
18. Thomas Jefferson to Wilson Cary Nicholas, Sept. 7, 1803, in Jefferson, *Writings* (New York: Library of America, 1984), 1140.
19. *McCulloch* v. *Maryland,* 4 Wheat. 316 (1819), at 407, 415.

20. *Home Building and Loan Assoc.* v. *Blaisdell*, 290 U.S. 398 (1934), at 443.
21. *Corfield* v. *Coryell*, 6 F.Cas. 546 (C.C.E.D.Pa., 1823), at 551.
22. *Slaughter-House Cases*, 16 Wall. 36 (1873).
23. *The Constitution of the United States of America: Analysis and Interpretation*, Annotations of Cases Decided by the Supreme Court of the United States to June 29, 1972 (Washington: Congressional Research Service, 1973), 1306.
24. *Roe* v. *Wade*, 410 U.S. 113 (1973), at 153.
25. *Bowers* v. *Hardwick*, 478 U.S. 186 (1986), at 199ff.
26. Roscoe Pound, "Introduction," in Russell B. Patterson, *The Forgotten Ninth Amendment* (Indianapolis: Bobbs-Merrill, 1955), iii, iv.

Chapter 2
Charles A. Lofgren

1. *Slaughter-House Cases*, 16 Wall. 36 (1873).
2. *Plessy* v. *Ferguson*, 163 U.S. 537 (1896).
3. David P. Currie, *The Constitution in the Supreme Court: The Second Century* (Chicago: University of Chicago Press, 1990), 40.
4. Act 118, Laws of Louisiana, 1869. See generally Mitchell Franklin, "The Foundations and Meaning of the Slaughterhouse Cases," *Tulane Law Review* 18 (1943): 1–88, 218–63; Ronald M. Labbe, "New Light on the Slaughterhouse Monopoly Act of 1869," in Edward F. Haas, ed., *Louisiana's Legal Heritage* (Pensacola, Fla.: Perdido Bay Press, 1983), 129–41.
5. Louisiana Supreme Court Transcript in *Durbridge* v. *The Slaughterhouse Company*, 27 La. Ann. 676 (1875), at 409, quoted in Franklin, "Foundations and Meaning," 25.
6. Franklin, "Foundations and Meaning," 1–20, 29–33.
7. Quoted in Labbe, "New Light on Slaughterhouse," 151.
8. *Live-Stock Dealers' and Butchers' Association* v. *Crescent City Live-Stock Landing & Slaughter-House Company*, 15 Fed. Cases 649, 649–51 (C.C.D.La., 1870)(Case No. 8,408)(June 10–11, 1870)(hereafter *Live-Stock Dealers* v. *Crescent City*). Actually, this was Bradley's *third* judicial encounter with the dispute. Besides having allowed the writ of error from the Louisiana Supreme Court (the first encounter), on June 3, 1870, just a week before the hearing on the Eighth District Court's new injunction, he had ruled in chambers against a request by the Crescent City Company to increase the bond required from the butchers in order for the writ of error to act as a stay on new state proceedings and existing orders in the cases covered by the writ of error. He held that once the writ was allowed, only the U.S. Supreme Court held jurisdiction.
9. *Live-Stock Dealers* v. *Crescent City*, at 650.
10. Ibid., at 652.
11. Ibid., at 650, 655.
12. Ibid., at 654-55.
13. *Slaughter-House Cases*, 10 Wall. 273 (1870). Justice Bradley dissented.
14. Charles Fairman, *Reconstruction and Reunion, 1864-1868*, Part One, vol. 6 of *The Oliver Wendell Holmes Devise History of the Supreme Court of the United States* (New

York: Macmillan, 1971), 1339–42; *Slaughter-House Cases,* 16 Wall. 36 (1873), at 58 [hereafter cited as *Slaughter-House Cases* (1873)].

15. Walton H. Hamilton, "The Path of Due Process of Law," in Conyers Read, ed., *The Constitution Reconsidered* (1938; rev. ed., New York: Harper and Row, 1968), 172. Walton was indulging in lawyerly license in saying the Fourteenth Amendment had at that time "drawn forth no judicial utterance"; lower courts had addressed it.

16. 21 L.Ed. at 402.

17. *Slaughter-House Cases* (1873), at 74.

18. Ibid., at 77–79.

19. Ibid., at 80.

20. Ibid., at 94–96.

21. Ibid., at 110-11.

22. Ibid., at 114, 119-21, 123-24.

23. Ibid., at 127.

24. Ibid., at 127, 129.

25. Ibid., at 67.

26. Robert H. Bork, *The Tempting of America: The Political Seduction of the Law* (New York: The Free Press, 1990), 36–39.

27. *Slaughter-House Cases* (1873), at 71–72.

28. Ibid., at 78.

29. *Congressional Globe,* 39th Cong., 1st sess., at 2766 (May 23, 1866).

30. Ibid.

31. Ibid., at 2765. Howard omitted some of the guarantees of the Bill of Rights from his listing, but he began the listing with "such as." In any event, the omissions were largely covered in Justice Washington's listing of fundamental rights, which Howard had already quoted.

32. Earl M. Maltz, *Civil Rights, the Constitution, and Congress, 1863-1869* (Lawrence: University Press of Kansas, 1990).

33. Paul Kens, "Whose Intent and Which Purpose? The Origins of the Fourteenth Amendment," *Reviews in American History* 20 (1992): 59, 61.

34. Maltz, *Civil Rights,* 117–18.

35. *Slaughter-House Cases* (1873), at 111, 105.

36. Ibid., at 114 (Bradley, closely paraphrasing Justice Washington in *Corfield* v. *Coryell*).

37. Ibid., at 110 and n. 1.

38. For other examples of recent assessments in addition to Maltz's *Civil Rights,* see William E. Nelson, *The Fourteenth Amendment: From Political Principle to Judicial Doctrine* (Cambridge: Harvard University Press, 1988), 110–64; Michael Kent Curtis, *No State Shall Abridge: The Fourteenth Amendment and the Bill of Rights* (Durham, N.C.: Duke University Press, 1986), 57–170; and Herman Belz, *Emancipation and Equal Rights: Politics and Constitutionalism in the Civil War Era* (New York: W. W. Norton, 1978), 115–22, 137–38. Also worth revisiting is the debate between Charles Fairman and William W. Crosskey over whether the Fourteenth Amendment was intended to incorporate the guarantees of the Bill of Rights. See Fairman, "Does the Fourteenth Amendment Incorporate the Bill of Rights? The Original Understanding," *Stanford Law Review* 2 (1949): 1–139; Crosskey, "Charles Fairman, 'Legislative History,' and the Constitutional Limitations on State Authority," *University of Chicago Law Review*

22 (1954): 2–119. Alfred Avins, himself a highly prolific "originalist" on the subject of the Fourteenth Amendment, gave the nod in the debate to Crosskey and incorporation in Avins, "Incorporation of the Bill of Rights: The Crosskey-Fairman Debates Revisited," *Harvard Journal of Legislation* 6 (1968): 1–26.

39. See Fairman, *Reconstruction and Reunion*, 1322.

40. *Slaughter-House Cases* (1873), at 67–68.

41. But for a scenario suggesting by implication that we cannot be at all certain that different outcomes in either *Slaughter-House* or *Plessy* would have made much difference, see Daniel Farber's comic-serious spoof, " 'Terminator 2½': The Constitution in an Alternate World," *Constitutional Commentary* 9 (1992): 59–73.

42. *Plessy v. Ferguson*, 163 U.S. 537.

43. This along with the following background and contextual material on *Plessy* is adapted from Charles A. Lofgren, *The Plessy Case: A Legal-Historical Interpretation* (New York: Oxford University Press, 1987), 7–43.

44. *Civil Rights Cases*, 109 U.S. 3 (1883).

45. *Plessy v. Ferguson*, at 542–43.

46. Ibid., at 543.

47. Ibid., at 549–50.

48. Ibid., at 550.

49. Ibid., at 550–51.

50. Ibid., at 544.

51. Ibid., at 544; emphasis added.

52. Ibid., at 551–52.

53. Ibid., at 551.

54. Ibid., at 554.

55. Ibid., at 555.

56. Ibid., at 556; quoting *Strauder v. West Virginia*, 100 U.S. 303 (1880), at 306–7.

57. *Plessy v. Ferguson*, at 557.

58. See ibid., at 558–59, and Lofgren, *The Plessy Case*, 193.

59. *Plessy v. Ferguson*, at 559.

60. Ibid., at 563.

61. Ibid., at 564.

62. Brown also noted Plessy's due-process claim that by giving conductors the authority to determine the race of passengers in making seat assignments, the act gave conductors the power to make judicial determinations. Brown declined to decide it, however, holding that the issue did not arise upon the actual record of the case, and he did not specifically use the phrase "due process" in connection with the claim. Ibid., at 549.

63. Ibid., at 543.

64. Ibid., at 544.

65. Ibid., at 551.

66. *Holden v. Hardy*, 169 U.S. 366 (1898), at 385. This decision upheld Utah's eight-hour law for miners as a valid police measure. In his opinion for the Court, Brown noted the newly understood physiological effects of working in mining, refining, and smelting operations. Ibid., at 394, 396.

67. Lofgren, *The Plessy Case*, 99–111 (on Brinton specifically, see 104–5).

68. *Plessy v. Ferguson*, at 555.

69. Ibid., at 560.

70. *Pace* v. *Alabama,* 106 U.S. 583 (1883). Harlan made better use of case law when he probed the status of railways as quasi-public agencies. Compare *Plessy* v. *Ferguson,* at 553–54, with Harry N. Scheiber, "Property Law, Expropriation, and Resource Allocation by Government, 1789–1910," *Journal of Economic History* 33 (1973): 232–51.

71. *Plessy* v. *Ferguson,* respectively at 557–58, 562–63, and 559–60.

72. Ibid., at 563–64.

73. For a complementary argument, and one that has stimulated my thinking relating to this and the following three paragraphs, see Hadley Arkes, *Beyond the Constitution* (Princeton: Princeton University Press, 1992), 51–55.

74. *Plessy* v. *Ferguson,* at 563, emphasis added.

75. Brief for Homer Plessy as Plaintiff in Error [submitted by Albion Tourgee and James C. Walker and filed April 6, 1896], *Plessy* v. *Ferguson,* at 34–35; partly quoted in Lofgren, *The Plessy Case,* 158, which also places the comments in the context of Tourgee's overall argument. The quotation is from the section of the brief specifically signed by Tourgee.

76. Abraham Lincoln, "Fragment on the Constitution and the Union" [ca. January 1861], in *The Collected Works of Abraham Lincoln,* ed. Roy P. Basler, vol. 4 (New Brunswick, N.J.: Rutgers University Press, 1953), 169.

77. See, for example, his dissent in *Lochner* v. *New York,* 198 U.S. 45 (1905).

Chapter 3

HADLEY ARKES

1. *Associated Press* v. *National Labor Relations Board,* 301 U.S. 103 (1937).

2. Ibid., at 140–41.

3. Ibid., at 140.

4. *Adair* v. *United States,* 208 U.S. 161 (1908).

5. *In re Higgins,* 27 F. 443 (1886), cited by Bernard Siegan, *Economic Liberties and the Constitution* (Chicago: University of Chicago Press, 1980), 124, 351.

6. 30 Stat. 424, c. 370.

7. *Adair* v. *United States,* at 168.

8. Ibid., at 172.

9. Lincoln had remarked that the black man might not be his social equal, but in his right not to be ruled without his consent and his "right to eat the bread, without leave of anybody else, which his own hand earns, *he is my equal and . . . the equal of every living man*" (*The Collected Works of Abraham Lincoln,* ed. Roy P. Basler, vol. 3 [New Brunswick, N.J.: Rutgers University Press, 1953], 16; italics in original). Lincoln might not wish to have a black woman as his wife, but he would respect her natural right to herself, and to the fruits of her own labor.

10. *Adair* v. *United States,* at 174–75.

11. Ibid., at 174.

12. Ibid., at 175.

13. Ibid., at 178.

14. *Labor Board* v. *Jones & Laughlin Steel Corp.,* 301 U.S. 1 (1937), at 98.

15. Ibid., at 97–98.

16. *Adair* v. *United States,* at 179.

17. *Coppage* v. *Kansas,* 236 U.S. 1 (1915), at 26–27.

18. Ibid., at 17.

19. Ibid.

20. Ibid., at 15.

21. *Lochner* v. *New York,* 198 U.S. 45 (1905), at 53.

22. See *Coppage* v. *Kansas,* at 11–13.

23. Ibid., at 19–20.

24. Ibid., at 19.

25. Ibid., at 20.

26. Ibid.

27. Most notably, Richard Epstein in his new book *Forbidden Grounds: The Case Against Employment Discrimination Laws* (Cambridge: Harvard University Press, 1992).

28. *Civil Rights Cases,* 109 U.S. 3 (1883), at 26–62.

29. *Coppage* v. *Kansas,* at 33.

30. Ibid., at 35.

31. Ibid., at 37.

32. *Civil Rights Cases,* at 59.

33. Ibid.

34. Ibid., at 40.

35. Ibid., at 41.

36. *Munn* v. *Illinois,* 94 U.S. 113 (1877).

37. Ibid., at 138.

38. *Civil Rights Cases,* at 26.

39. See my book *The Philosopher in the City* (Princeton: Princeton University Press, 1981), 240–42.

40. For a fuller statement of this argument, see my book *First Things* (Princeton: Princeton University Press, 1986), chap. 15, especially 355–57.

Chapter 4
AKHIL REED AMAR

1. *Patterson* v. *Colorado,* 205 U.S. 454 (1907).

2. On the historic connection between jury trial and freedom of the press, see Akhil Reed Amar, "The Bill of Rights as a Constitution," *Yale Law Journal* 100 (1991): 1131, 1150–51.

3. *Patterson* v. *Colorado,* at 462.

4. *Gitlow* v. *New York,* 268 U.S. 652 (1925), at 666. ("For present purposes we may and do assume that freedom of speech and of the press—which are protected by the First Amendment from abridgment by Congress—are among the fundamental personal rights and 'liberties' protected by the due process clause of the Fourteenth Amendment from impairment by the States.")

5. For an outstanding discussion and analysis of *Patterson* and its fascinating facts, see Lucas A. Powe, Jr., *The Fourth Estate and the Constitution* (Berkeley: University of California Press, 1991), 1–16.

6. For more elaboration of why it is downright silly to limit the First Amendment to a mere ban on prior restraint, see Akhil Reed Amar, "The Bill of Rights and the Fourteenth Amendment," *Yale Law Journal* 101 (1992): 1193, 1266–68. What's more, as I have shown elsewhere (see Amar, "The Bill of Rights as a Constitution," 1150–51), a key purpose of the prior-restraint rule was to interpose a jury in cases between government officials and the press—a point utterly lost on the *Patterson* Court, which upheld a censorship that, like prior restraint, cut the jury out of the loop.

7. On the significance of the Preamble to proper constitutional interpretation at the founding, see H. Jefferson Powell, "The Original Understanding of Original Intent," *Harvard Law Review* 98 (1985), 885, 899, 915, 923 n. 205, 942–43.

8. For more discussion, see Akhil Reed Amar, "The Central Meaning of Republican Government: Popular Sovereignty, Majority Rule, and the Denominator Problem," *University of Colorado Law Review*, forthcoming 1994.

9. See Amar, "The Bill of Rights and the Fourteenth Amendment," 1242.

10. See Charles L. Black, Jr., *Structure and Relationship in Constitutional Law* (Woodbridge, Conn.: Ox Bow Press, 1969), 42–51.

11. *Patterson v. Colorado,* at 464 (emphasis added).

12. For more elaboration of the declaratory theory, see Amar, "The Bill of Rights and the Fourteenth Amendment," 1205–12.

13. Elsewhere I have developed this argument, and the evidence behind it, at great length. See generally Amar, "The Bill of Rights and the Fourteenth Amendment." But I do not believe that the Fourteenth Amendment mechanically incorporated all clauses of the Bill of Rights. Rather, I have tried to develop a model of "refined incorporation" that synthesizes the divergent approaches of Justices Black, Brennan, and Frankfurter (total incorporation, selective incorporation, and ordered liberty/fundamental fairness, respectively). I have summarized my position as follows:

> This synthesis, which I call "refined incorporation," begins with Black's insight that *all* of the privileges and immunities of citizens recognized in the Bill of Rights became applicable *against* states by dint of the Fourteenth Amendment. But not all of the provisions of the original Bill of Rights were indeed rights of citizens. Some instead were at least in part rights of states, and as such, awkward to incorporate fully against states. Most obvious, of course, is the Tenth Amendment, but other provisions of the first eight amendments resembled the Tenth much more than Justice Black admitted. Thus, there is deep wisdom in Justice Brennan's invitation to consider incorporation clause by clause rather than wholesale. But having identified the right unit of analysis, Brennan posed the wrong question: Is a given provision of the original Bill really a *fundamental* right? The right question is whether the provision really guarantees a privilege or immunity of individual citizens rather than a right of states or the public at large. And when we ask this question, clause by clause, we must be attentive to the possibility, flagged by Frankfurter, that a particular principle in the Bill of Rights may change its shape in the process of absorption into the Fourteenth Amendment. This change can occur for reasons rather different from those offered by Frankfurter, who diverted attention from the right question by his jaundiced view of much of the original Bill and by his utter disregard of the language and history of the privileges or immunities clause. Certain hybrid provisions of the original Bill—part citizen right, part state right—may need to shed their state-

right husk before their citizen-right core can be absorbed by the Fourteenth Amendment. Other provisions may become less majoritarian and populist, and more libertarian, as they are repackaged in the Fourteenth Amendment as liberal civil rights — "privileges or immunities" of individuals — rather than republican political "right[s] of the people," as in the original Bill. [Ibid., 1197]

14. For more discussion of this context, and documentation of all my claims in this paragraph, see Amar, "The Bill of Rights and the Fourteenth Amendment."

15. *Bolling* v. *Sharpe*, 347 U.S. 497 (1954).

16. *Brown* v. *Board of Education*, 347 U.S. 483 (1954).

17. *Bolling* v. *Sharpe*, at 500.

18. Ibid. (emphasis added).

19. See Charles Black, "The Lawfulness of the Segregation Decisions," *Yale Law Journal* 69 (1960): 421.

20. *Dred Scott* v. *Sandford*, 60 U.S. (19 How.) 393 (1857), at 571–88.

21. *Congressional Globe*, 39th Cong., 1st Sess., at 474 (1866).

22. *Civil Rights Cases*, 109 U.S. 3 (1883), at 32–43.

23. *Plessy* v. *Ferguson*, 163 U.S. 537 (1896), at 562–64.

24. *Civil Rights Cases*, at 48.

25. *Gibson* v. *Mississippi*, 162 U.S. 565 (1896), at 591.

26. See also *Maxwell* v. *Dow*, 176 U.S. 581 (1900), at 605–17, and *Twining* v. *New Jersey*, 211 U.S. 78 (1908), at 114–27.

27. *Plessy* v. *Ferguson*, at 560.

28. See Amar, "The Bill of Rights and the Fourteenth Amendment," 1224–26, 1233–34.

29. See ibid., 1234 n. 187, and sources cited therein.

30. *Congressional Globe*, 39th Cong., 1st Sess., at 1034.

31. Ibid.

32. Howard Jay Graham, *Everyman's Constitution* (Madison: State Historical Society of Wisconsin, 1968), 57 n. 87.

33. Pennsylvania Constitution of 1776 (Declaration of Rights), art. VIII.

34. In articles 10, IX, X, and XII, respectively.

35. Thomas Cooley, *A Treatise on the Constitutional Limitations Which Rest Upon the Legislative Power of the States of the American Union*, ★353.

36. *Dartmouth College* v. *Woodward*, 17 U.S. (4 Wheat.) 518 (1819), at 581.

37. See also Earl M. Maltz, *Civil Rights, the Constitution, and Congress, 1863-1869* (Lawrence: University Press of Kansas, 1990), 98–99; Rodney C. Mott, *Due Process of Law* (Indianapolis: Bobbs-Merrill, 1926), 256–99; Earl Maltz, "Fourteenth Amendment Concepts in the Antebellum Era," *American Journal of Legal History* 32 (1988): 305, 317, 326; Mark A. Graber, "A Constitutional Conspiracy Unmasked: Why 'No State' Does Not Mean 'No State,'" *Constitutional Commentary* 10 (1993): 87.

38. *Gibson* v. *Mississippi*, at 591.

39. Ibid.

Chapter 5
NADINE STROSSEN

1. *Calder* v. *Bull*, 3 Dall. 386 (1798).

2. See generally Gerald Gunther, *Constitutional Law*, 12th ed. (Westbury, N.Y.: Foundation Press, 1991), 439–65.

3. Ibid., 411–31.

4. See, e.g., *Whitney* v. *California*, 274 U.S. 357 (1927), at 375 (Brandeis, concurring): "Those who won our independence believed that the final end of the State was to make men free. . . ."

5. In an early case, *Truax* v. *Raich*, 239 U.S. 33 (1915), predating its virtual rubber-stamp approval of economic regulations, the Court affirmed the intimate connection between pursuing one's profession and personal liberty:

> It requires no argument to show that the right to work for a living in the common occupation of the community is of the very essence of the personal freedom and opportunity that it was the purpose of the [Fourteenth] Amendment to secure. [41]

6. *Griswold* v. *Connecticut*, 381 U.S. 479 (1965).

7. Ibid., at 481–82:

> [W]e are met with a wide range of questions that implicate the Due Process Clause of the Fourteenth Amendment. Overtones of some arguments suggest that *Lochner* v. *New York* . . . should be our guide. But we decline that invitation. . . .

8. Ibid., at 482–85.

9. *Ferguson* v. *Skrupa*, 372 U.S. 726 (1963).

10. See, e.g., *Duncan* v. *Louisiana*, 391 U.S. 145 (1968), at 162 (Black, joined by Douglas, dissenting); *Adamson* v. *California*, 332 U.S. 46 (1947), at 68 (Black, joined by Douglas, dissenting).

11. See *Griswold* v. *Connecticut*, at 500 (emphasis in original):

> [W]hat I find implicit in the Court's opinion is that the "incorporation" doctrine may be used to *restrict* the reach of Fourteenth Amendment Due Process. For me this is just as unacceptable constitutional doctrine as is the use of the "incorporation" approach to *impose* upon the States all the requirements of the Bill of Rights. . . .

12. Ibid., at 485–86.

13. Ibid.

14. See Brief of the United States as Amicus Curiae Supporting Appellants at 12, *Webster* v. *Reproductive Health Services*, 492 U.S. 490 (1989) (no. 88–605) (stating that *Griswold* is a case "rooted in . . . freedom from unreasonable searches assured by the Fourth Amendment"); Brief of the United States as Amicus Curiae in Support of Appellants at 28, *Thornburgh* v. *American College of Obstetricians & Gynecologists*, 476 U.S. 747 (1986) (nos. 84-495 and 84-1379) (suggesting that "Fourth Amendment policies . . . provide . . . support for the holding in" *Griswold*).

15. *Griswold* v. *Connecticut*, at 487.

16. Ibid., at 502, quoting *Prince* v. *Massachusetts,* 321 U.S. 158 (1944), at 166.

17. Ibid., at 503, quoting *Kovacs* v. *Cooper,* 336 U.S. 77 (1949), at 95. Justice Douglas's majority opinion drew a similar distinction:

> We do not sit as a super-legislature to determine the wisdom, need, and propriety of laws that touch economic problems, business affairs, or social conditions. This law, however, operates directly on an intimate relation of husband and wife. . . . [482]

18. See *Bowers* v. *Hardwick,* 478 U.S. 186 (1986), at 190–91.

19. *Griswold* v. *Connecticut,* at 527.

20. Ibid., at 528.

21. Ibid., at 499.

22. See, e.g., *Griffin* v. *California,* 380 U.S. 609 (1965), at 615; *Pointer* v. *Texas,* 380 U.S. 400 (1965), at 408.

23. *Griswold* v. *Connecticut,* at 500, quoting *Palko* v. *Connecticut,* 302 U.S. 319 (1937), at 325.

24. *Poe* v. *Ullman,* 367 U.S. 497 (1961), at 522.

25. Ibid.

26. See generally Nadine Strossen, "Justice Harlan and the Bill of Rights: A Model for How a Classic Conservative Court Would Enforce the Bill of Rights," *New York Law School Law Review* 36 (1991): 133 (drawing contrasts between Harlan's rulings on the Bill of Rights and those of Chief Justice Rehnquist and his allies on the current Supreme Court, and showing that the latter's hostility toward the judicial protection of human rights sets them apart from Justice Harlan's classic conservatism).

27. For Bork's critique of *Griswold,* see Robert Bork, "Neutral Principles and Some First Amendment Problems," *Indiana Law Journal* 47 (1971): 1. During the hearings on his nomination to the Supreme Court, Bork attempted to temper this prior denunciation of *Griswold.* He said that his criticism was of the Court's rationale, and that if the case were presented to him he would consider another rationale for invalidating Connecticut's anti-contraceptive law. When pressed to suggest such an alternative rationale, though, Judge Bork said he had not given the matter enough thought. See *Hearings before the Committee on the Judiciary of the United States Senate on the Nomination of Robert H. Bork to be Associate Justice of the Supreme Court of the United States,* Sept. 16, 1987, at 3789 (comment of Sen. Specter).

28. See *Griswold* v. *Connecticut,* at 522–26 (Black, dissenting).

29. *Calder* v. *Bull,* 3 Dall. 386 (1798).

30. *Adamson* v. *California,* 332 U.S. 46 (1947).

31. See *Griswold* v. *Connecticut,* at 507.

32. Ibid., at 478–79.

33. See, e.g., *Adamson* v. *California,* at 90–92.

34. *Griswold* v. *Connecticut,* at 511.

35. Ibid., at 524.

36. Ibid., at 519.

37. Ibid., at 522.

38. Ibid., at 524.

39. Ibid., at 510.

40. *Poe* v. *Ullman,* at 542–43.

41. See Stephen Macedo, *The New Right v. The Constitution* (Washington, D.C.: Cato Institute, 1987), 32.

42. *Poe v. Ullman,* at 540.

43. *McCulloch v. Maryland,* 4 Wheat. 316 (1819).

44. *Poe v. Ullman,* at 540.

45. *Calder v. Bull,* 3 Dall. 386 (1798).

46. *Poe v. Ullman,* at 542 (emphasis added).

47. Ibid.

48. Ibid., at 540.

49. *Roe v. Wade,* 410 U.S. 113 (1973), at 172–73.

50. Ibid., at 167–68.

51. *Poe v. Ullman,* at 542–43.

52. Ibid., at 544.

53. *Griswold v. Connecticut,* at 529.

54. *Poe v. Ullman,* at 540.

55. Ibid., at 551, quoting *Weems v. United States,* 217 U.S. 349 (1910), at 373.

56. *Griswold v. Connecticut,* at 500–501.

57. See ibid., at 501, citing *Wesberry v. Sanders,* 376 U.S. 1 (1964), and *Reynolds v. Sims,* 377 U.S. 533 (1964).

58. *Roe v. Wade,* 410 U.S. 113 (1973).

59. Ibid., at 153.

60. Ibid., at 756.

61. See ibid., at 153–54, 162.

62. Ibid., at 167–68.

63. See ibid., at 758, n. 4. See also the relevant passage from Douglas's *Griswold* opinion quoted above in note 17.

64. See *Griswold v. Connecticut,* at 503 (marriage "'come[s] to this Court with a momentum for respect lacking when appeal is made to liberties which derive merely from shifting economic arrangements'").

65. For a critique of this dichotomy, see e.g., Robert McCloskey, "Economic Due Process and the Supreme Court: An Exhumation and Reburial," *Supreme Court Review* 34 (1962): 45–50. For a defense, see, e.g., Archibald Cox, "The Supreme Court, 1965 Term—Foreword: Constitutional Adjudication and the Promotion of Human Rights," *Harvard Law Review* 80 (1966): 91.

66. *Lynch v. Household Finance Corp.,* 405 U.S. 538 (1972), at 552.

67. See Nadine Strossen, *"Michigan Department of State Police v. Sitz:* A Roadblock to Meaningful Enforcement of Constitutional Rights," *Hastings Law Journal* 42 (1991): 285, 366–69. This development is summarized as follows:

> The Rehnquist Court's adoption of a rational basis test for evaluating claimed personal rights infringements parallels an earlier Court's move toward such a deferential standard of review regarding claimed economic rights infringements, thus ending the so-called *"Lochner* era. . . ." [366–67]

68. *Roe v. Wade,* at 210.

69. Ibid., at 210–11.

70. Ibid., at 211–13.

71. *Jacobson v. Massachusetts,* 197 U.S. 11 (1905); quoted in *Roe v. Wade,* at 213–14.

72. See *Bowers* v. *Hardwick*, at 203–6.

73. See Elizabeth M. Schneider, "Commentary: The Affirmative Dimensions of Douglas's Privacy," in Stephen L. Wasby, ed., *He Shall Not Pass This Way Again: The Legacy of Justice William O. Douglas* (Pittsburgh: University of Pittsburgh Press, 1990).

74. See, e.g., Rhonda Copelon, "Unpacking Patriarchy: Reproduction, Sexuality, Originalism and Constitutional Change," in Jules Lobel, ed., *A Less Than Perfect Union: Alternative Perspectives on the U.S. Constitution* (New York: Monthly Review Press, 1988); Sylvia Law, "Rethinking Sex and the Constitution," *University of Pennsylvania Law Review* 132 (1984): 956; Janice Goodman, Rhonda Copelon Schoenbrod, and Nancy Stearns, "*Roe* and *Doe*: Where Do We Go From Here?," *Women's Rights Law Reporter* 20 (1973): 1.

75. See *Roe* v. *Wade*, at 215–16:

> The vicissitudes of life produce pregnancies which may be unwanted, or which may impair "health" in the broad . . . sense of the term, or which may imperil the life of the mother, or which in the full setting of the case may create such suffering, dislocations, misery, or tragedy as to make an early abortion the only civilized step to take.

76. See ibid., at 221, 222, where, in addition to using *convenience* twice in the passage quoted in the text (at note 77), White also says:

> The Court apparently values the convenience of the pregnant woman more than the continued existence and development of the life or potential life that she carries. . . .
> It is my view . . . that the Texas statute is not constitutionally infirm because it denies abortions to those who seek to serve only their convenience. . . .

77. Ibid., at 221.

78. Ibid., at 222.

79. *Bowers* v. *Hardwick*, at 194.

80. Ibid., at 194–95.

81. *Roe* v. *Wade*, at 173.

82. See Strossen, *"Michigan Department of State Police* v. *Sitz,"* 364.

83. *Roe* v. *Wade*, at 174.

84. See Strossen, "The Supreme Court's Role: Guarantor of Individual and Minority Group Rights," *University of Richmond Law Review* 26 (1992): 467.

85. *West Virginia Board of Education* v. *Barnette*, 319 U.S. 624 (1943), at 638.

86. *Roe* v. *Wade*, at 173.

87. See Erwin Chemerinsky, "Foreword: Our Vanishing Constitution," *Harvard Law Review* 103 (1989): 43; Nadine Strossen, "Recent U.S. and International Judicial Protection of Individual Rights: A Comparative Legal Process Analysis and Proposed Synthesis," *Hastings Law Journal* 41 (1990): 805, 866–903.

88. *Bowers* v. *Hardwick*, 478 U.S. 186 (1986).

89. See Michael Hardwick, "What Are You Doing in My Bedroom?," in Peter Irons, ed., *The Courage of Their Convictions* (New York: Penguin, 1988), 396.

90. *Bowers* v. *Hardwick*, at 190.

91. Ibid., at 200.

92. Ibid., at 199, quoting *Olmstead* v. *United States,* 277 U.S. 438 (1928), at 478 (Brandeis, dissenting).

93. *Pierce* v. *Society of Sisters,* 268 U.S. 510 (1925).

94. *Meyer* v. *Nebraska,* 262 U.S. 390 (1923).

95. *Prince* v. *Massachusetts,* 321 U.S. 158 (1944).

96. *Skinner* v. *Oklahoma,* 316 U.S. 535 (1942).

97. *Loving* v. *Virginia,* 388 U.S. 1 (1967).

98. *Eisenstadt* v. *Baird,* 405 U.S. 438 (1972).

99. *Bowers* v. *Hardwick,* at 190.

100. Ibid., at 190–91.

101. Ibid., at 204–5 (citations omitted; emphasis in original).

102. *Stanley* v. *Georgia,* 394 U.S. 557 (1969).

103. *Bowers* v. *Hardwick,* at 195.

104. Ibid., at 207–8.

105. *Stanley* v. *Georgia,* at 565.

106. *Bowers* v. *Hardwick,* at 208.

107. See ibid., at 214–16. The correct understanding of legal history as banning *all* sodomy posed, in Stevens's view, two questions regarding the constitutionality of the Georgia statute, both of which he answered negatively:

> Because the Georgia statute expresses the traditional view that sodomy is . . . immoral . . . regardless of the identity of the persons who engage in it, I believe that a proper analysis of its constitutionality requires consideration of two questions: First, may a State totally prohibit the described conduct by means of a neutral law applying without exception to all persons . . . ? If not, may the State save the statute by announcing that it will only enforce the law against homosexuals? [216]

108. Ibid., at 206.

109. See Laurence Tribe, *American Constitutional Law,* 2d ed. (Mineola, N.Y.: Foundation Press, 1988), secs. 15–21, at 1428.

110. Anne B. Goldstein, "History, Homosexuality, and Political Values: Searching for the Hidden Determinants of *Bowers* v. *Hardwick,*" *Yale Law Journal* 97 (1988): 1073.

111. See *Bowers* v. *Hardwick,* at 196 (in upholding the statute, the majority relied on "the presumed belief of a majority of the Georgia electorate that homosexual sodomy is immoral and unacceptable").

112. See ibid., at 209 ("Nothing in the record . . . provides any justification for finding the activity forbidden by [the Georgia statute] to be physically dangerous, either to the persons engaged in it or to others"). Justice Stevens's dissent also reflects the assumption that some actual harm would have to be shown to justify the statute. See ibid., at 217–18.

113. See Goldstein, "History, Homosexuality, and Political Values":

> *Bowers* v. *Hardwick* . . . really turn[s] on the Justices' unstated disagreements over fundamental political values. The majority applied classical conservative principles, permitting Georgia to justify its statute by its congruence with traditional moral views. It grounded this argument in the Constitution by equating "tradition" with the views of the Founders. [1102]

114. *Barnes* v. *Glen Theatre,* 115 L.Ed. 2d 504 (1991).

115. See ibid., at 504 (Rehnquist, joined by O'Connor and Kennedy) and at 521 (Souter concurring in judgment).

116. See ibid., at 513 (plurality opinion) and at 517 (Scalia, concurring in judgment). Justice Scalia was the only member of the majority who sought to justify the nude dancing prohibition as advancing another societal interest—namely, preventing prostitution, sexual assault, and other criminal activity. See ibid., at 522. However, there was no evidence either that averting these "secondary effects" was the legislature's intent in banning public nudity, or that any such effects had occurred in conjunction with nude barroom dancing.

117. *Bowers* v. *Hardwick,* at 196.

118. Ibid.

119. *Poe* v. *Ullman,* at 545.

120. *Barnes* v. *Glen Theatre,* at 517.

121. Tribe, *American Constitutional Law,* 1428.

122. See *Bowers* v. *Hardwick,* at 199, 197 (Blackmun, dissenting); *Roe* v. *Wade,* at 152 (Blackmun's opinion for the Court); ibid., at 758 (Douglas, concurring); *Griswold* v. *Connecticut,* at 494 (Goldberg, concurring); and *Poe* v. *Ullman,* at 550 (Harlan, dissenting).

123. *Olmstead* v. *United States,* 277 U.S. 438 (1928), at 470–85 (Brandeis, dissenting).

124. *Katz* v. *United States,* 389 U.S. 347 (1967), at 353.

125. *Olmstead* v. *United States,* at 471–79.

Chapter 6

GERARD V. BRADLEY

1. *Planned Parenthood* v. *Casey,* 112 Sup. Ct. 2791 (1992).

2. *Lee* v. *Weisman,* 112 Sup. Ct. 2649 (1992).

3. *Planned Parenthood* v. *Casey,* at 2804.

4. "[N]or shall any state deprive any person of life, liberty, or property, without due process of law." Presumably, the federal government is bound to observe the same entitlements by virtue of the Fifth Amendment's Due Process Clause.

5. *Planned Parenthood* v. *Casey,* at 2804, quoting *Whitney* v. *California,* 274 U.S. 357 (1927), at 373 (Brandeis, concurring).

6. *Planned Parenthood* v. *Casey,* at 2804.

7. Ibid., at 2807.

8. Ibid.

9. Ibid.

10. *Lee* v. *Weisman,* at 2657.

11. *Planned Parenthood* v. *Casey,* at 2807.

12. Ibid.

13. *Webster* v. *Reproductive Health Services,* 492 U.S. 490 (1989), Brief for a Group of American Law Professors as Amicus Curiae in Support of Appellees.

14. *Planned Parenthood* v. *Casey,* at 2806.

15. *Lee* v. *Weisman,* at 2661.

16. *Planned Parenthood* v. *Casey*, at 2820.

17. William Brennan, "The Constitution of the United States: Contemporary Ratification," a speech delivered at Georgetown University on October 12, 1985. This presentation has been, I think accurately, taken as a summation of the liberal constitutionalism of the last twenty-five or so years, which culminated, in my view, in *Casey* and *Lee*.

18. *Planned Parenthood* v. *Casey*, at 2815.

19. See Gerard Bradley, *Church-State Relationships in America* (Westport, Conn.: Greenwood Press, 1987).

20. Joseph Raz, "Authority, Law and Morality," *The Monist* 68 (July 1985): 295.

21. Russell Hittinger, "Natural Law in the Positive Laws: A Legislative or Adjudicative Issue?," *Review of Politics*, vol. 55, no. 1 (Winter 1993): 12.

22. *Planned Parenthood* v. *Casey*, at 2806, quoting *Poe* v. *Ullman*, 367 U.S. 497 (1961), at 542 (Harlan, dissenting from dismissal on jurisdictional grounds).

23. Brennan, "Constitution of the United States."

24. Ibid. With the "majestic generalities" quotation in the first paragraph, Brennan cites *West Virginia Board of Education* v. *Barnette*, 319 U.S. 624 (1943), at 639.

25. Sidney Fine, *Frank Murphy: The Washington Years* (Ann Arbor: University of Michigan Press, 1984), 568.

26. Ibid., 568–69.

27. *Lee* v. *Weisman*, at 2666, n. 10.

28. Martin Marty, *Modern American Religion: The Noise of Conflict 1919-1941*, vol. 2 (Chicago: University of Chicago Press, 1991), 4.

29. *Planned Parenthood* v. *Casey*, at 2806.

30. *Lee* v. *Weisman*, at 2686.

31. *Michael H.* v. *Gerald D.*, 491 U.S. 110 (1987), at 141 (Brennan, dissenting).

Chapter 7
Mary Ann Glendon

1. Ludwig Wittgenstein, *Philosophical Investigations*, 3d ed., trans. G. E. M. Anscombe (Oxford: Basil Blackwell, 1967), 50.

2. It was not always thus. According to Paul Carrington, students in early American law schools were required to have a detailed knowledge of the Constitution, and *The Federalist* was often used as a basic text. Carrington, "Butterfly Effects: The Possibilities of Law Teaching in a Democracy," *Duke Law Journal* 41 (1992): 741, 759.

3. On this point, I have benefited greatly from works-in-progress by Professor Winfried Brugger of Heidelberg University: "Legal Interpretation, Schools of Jurisprudence, and Anthropology," and "Is There Something to Be Learned from German Constitutional Law?"

4. See, generally, Mary Ann Glendon, "The Sources of Law in a Changing Legal Order," *Creighton Law Review* 17 (1984): 663.

5. According to H. Jefferson Powell, the American framers initially were torn "between a global rejection of any and all methods of constitutional construction and a willingness to interpret the constitutional text in accordance with the common law principles that had been used to construe statutes." In the early years of the republic,

Powell says, the problem was resolved for a time when a consensus developed on "original intent." Powell, "The Original Understanding of Original Intent," *Harvard Law Review* 98 (1985): 885, 887. On Madison's rejection of the methods of the common law for the purpose of constitutional interpretation, see Gary McDowell, *Equity and the Constitution* (Chicago: University of Chicago Press, 1982), 55–60.

6. Cass R. Sunstein, review of *On Reading the Constitution* by Laurence H. Tribe and Michael C. Dorf, *The New Republic,* 11 March 1991, 35.

7. Roscoe Pound, "The Formative Era of American Law," in John Honnold, ed., *The Life of the Law* (London: Collier-MacMillan, 1964), 60.

8. See *Max Weber on Law in Economy and Society,* ed. Max Rheinstein (Cambridge: Harvard University Press, 1954), especially chap. 7.

9. For a detailed exposition, see Thomas Probst, *Die Aenderung der Rechtsprechung* (Basel: Helbing & Lichtenhahn, 1993).

10. Karl N. Llewellyn, *The Common Law Tradition* (Boston: Little, Brown, 1960), 379. As a legislative draftsman, Llewellyn borrowed freely from German models. Shael Herman, "Llewellyn the Civilian: Speculations on the Contribution of Continental Experience to the Uniform Commercial Code," *Tulane Law Review* 56 (1982): 1125, 1130 n. 20.

11. Llewellyn, *The Common Law Tradition,* 380.

12. See, generally, Mary Ann Glendon, Michael Gordon, and Christopher Osakwe, *Comparative Legal Traditions,* 2d ed. (St. Paul, Minn.: West Publishing Co., 1994), chap. 5.

13. See generally Glendon, "The Sources of Law," 666–73.

14. Pound, "The Formative Era of American Law," 59.

15. Glendon, "The Sources of Law," 667.

16. Grant Gilmore, *The Ages of American Law* (New Haven: Yale University Press, 1977), 63.

17. Lawrence Friedman, *A History of American Law,* 2d ed. (New York: Simon and Schuster, 1985), 122–23, 345. Though the Supreme Court claimed the power to have the last word on the meaning of the constitutional text in *Marbury* v. *Madison* (1803), it generally avoided direct confrontation with other branches of government until the late nineteenth century. In the first seventy-five years, only two federal laws were held unconstitutional (one was the Missouri compromise in *Dred Scott* v. *Sandford* [1857]). In the decade of the 1880s alone, however, the Court struck down five federal and forty-eight state laws. James Q. Wilson, *American Government: Institutions and Policies,* 5th ed. (Lexington, Mass.: D.C. Heath, 1992), 398.

18. Gilmore, *The Ages of American Law,* 66. See also Friedman, *A History of American Law,* 358–62.

19. Frankfurter, "Some Reflections on the Reading of Statutes," *Columbia Law Review* 47 (1947): 527.

20. Pound, "The Formative Era of American Law," 61.

21. See, e.g., Holmes's dissents in *Lochner* v. *New York,* 198 U.S. 45 (1905), at 74–76; *Adkins* v. *Children's Hospital,* 261 U.S. 525 (1923), at 570; and *Truax* v. *Corrigan,* 257 U.S. 312 (1921), at 344. See also McDowell, *Equity and the Constitution,* 128.

22. Cardozo, "A Ministry of Justice," *Harvard Law Review* 35 (1921): 113. The story is told in Henry Hart and Albert Sacks, *The Legal Process: Basic Problems in the Making and Application of Law* (Cambridge: mimeographed, 1958), 809–17.

23. Pound, "Common Law and Legislation," *Harvard Law Review* 21 (1908): 383; Landis, "Statutes and the Sources of Law," in *Harvard Legal Essays* (Cambridge: Harvard University Press, 1934), 213; Frankfurter, "Some Reflections on the Reading of Statutes," *Columbia Law Review* 47 (1947): 527; and Karl N. Llewellyn, *The Bramble Bush,* 3d ed. (Dobbs Ferry, N.Y.: Oceana, 1960). See also Llewellyn, *The Common Law Tradition*.

24. Hart and Sacks, *The Legal Process,* 1201.

25. J. Willard Hurst, *Dealing with Statutes* (New York: Columbia University Press, 1982), 1.

26. "Report of the Harvard Law School Comprehensive Curricular Assessment Committee," 5 May 1992, 4.

27. Laurence H. Tribe and Michael C. Dorf, *On Reading the Constitution* (Cambridge: Harvard University Press, 1991).

28. Ibid., 109.

29. While Tribe and Dorf nod in the direction of "structure," they use that term to mean, not federalism and separation of powers, but penumbras and emanations; e.g., "One way to go about identifying the central value or values implicit in a specific constitutional clause is to locate that clause within the overall structure of the rest of the Constitution—to ask whether the practices that are either mandated or proscribed by the Constitution presuppose some view without which these textual requirements are incoherent." Ibid., 59. Only rarely do Tribe and Dorf stray from the Bill of Rights to discuss the rest of the Constitution.

30. Ernst Freund, "Constitutional Law," in *Encyclopaedia of the Social Sciences,* vol. 4 (New York: Macmillan, 1937), 248–49.

31. See, e.g., the decisions of the German constitutional court collected in Donald Kommers, *The Constitutional Jurisprudence of the Federal Constitutional Court of Germany* (Durham, N.C.: Duke University Press, 1989); but Brugger (see note 3) makes the important point that the U.S. Constitution is much older than these others, and much less specific than, say, the German Basic Law of 1949.

32. Interestingly, original intent is treated as receding in significance with the age of a code or constitution. Thus French jurists treat the ideas and intentions of the drafters of the Civil Code of 1804 as almost irrelevant to the decision of present-day cases. Alfred Rieg, "Judicial Interpretation of Written Rules," in Glendon, Gordon, and Osakwe, *Comparative Legal Traditions,* 229–30. In a 1977 decision, the German Federal Constitutional Court declined to accord decisive weight to evidence of the intent of the framers of the 1949 Basic Law. Kommers, *The Constitutional Jurisprudence,* 316.

33. Amar, "The Bill of Rights as a Constitution," *Yale Law Journal* 100 (1991): 1131, and "The Bill of Rights and the Fourteenth Amendment," *Yale Law Journal* 101 (1992): 1193; John Hart Ely, *Democracy and Distrust* (Cambridge: Harvard University Press, 1980), 88–104; Michael McConnell, "Federalism: Evaluating the Founders' Design," *University of Chicago Law Review* 54 (1987): 1484; and Geoffrey Miller, "Rights and Structure in Constitutional Theory," *Social Philosophy and Policy* 8 (1991): 196.

34. See Bator, "The Constitution as Architecture: Legislative and Administrative Courts Under Article III," *Indiana Law Journal* 65 (1990): 233.

35. To many political scientists, lawyers' concentration on rights at the expense

of many other parts of our constitutional tradition has seemed odd. Much of the new structural legal scholarship represents a belated acknowledgment of Herbert Storing's observation:

> The Bill of Rights provides a fitting close to the parenthesis around the Constitution that the preamble opens. But the substance is a design of government with powers to act and a structure to make it act wisely and responsibly. It is in that design, not in its preamble or its epilogue, that the security of the American civil and political liberty lies. [Herbert J. Storing, "The Constitution and the Bill of Rights," in *Essays on the Constitution,* ed. M. Judd Harmon (Port Washington, N.Y.: Kennikat Press, 1978), 48.]

36. Miller, "Rights and Structure," 198, n. 41.

37. See, e.g., *Williamson* v. *Lee Optical Co.,* 348 U.S. 483 (1955), at 488; *Ferguson* v. *Skrupa,* 372 U.S. 726 (1963); *Hawaii Housing* v. *Midkiff,* 467 U.S. 229 (1983), at 240–41.

38. From the last clause of the Fifth Amendment: "nor shall private property be taken for public use, without just compensation."

39. Much of that mistrust derives from the fact that racially discriminatory legislation was common in many parts of the United States until the 1960s. However, the dramatic success of lawsuits attacking such legislation seems to have fostered a taste for litigation and for all-or-nothing victories, deflecting reformist energy from the ordinary democratic processes that are better suited for ordinary controversies.

40. Regarding disincentives that keep many law professors from participating in ordinary politics, Paul Carrington has written (with deliberate irony):

> [O]ne must associate with persons who are not always members of an elite. One must go to meetings and not only talk, but also listen politely, often more than once to the same bad idea. One must study and think about issues and problems that are of immediate concern to others, and not only those issues most attractive to one's own interests. . . . To be effective, one must compromise and accommodate. . . . One must risk the sting of visible defeat. . . . [O]ne must sometimes first win trust by bearing the most unwelcome burdens, performing prosaic tasks that do less honor to one's talents than one might wish. . . . [Paul D. Carrington, "Aftermath," in P. Cane and J. Stapleton, eds., *Essays for Patrick Atiyah* (Oxford: Clarendon Press, 1991), 113, 140.]

Index of Names

177

LEADING PROFESSORS and practitioners of the law here reflect on how America's Supreme Court justices have gone about the task of interpreting the Constitution.

WALTER BERNS surveys the Court's constitutional approach during its first decades. CHARLES LOFGREN examines some early interpretations of the Fourteenth Amendment. HADLEY ARKES considers the constitutional structure of privacy. AKHIL AMAR deals with the debate over incorporation and reverse incorporation. NADINE STROSSEN looks at the modern understanding of constitutional privacy. GERARD BRADLEY finds a proposed "new constitution" in recent Court decisions. Finally, MARY ANN GLENDON appeals for a structural approach to constitutional interpretation.

The writers ground their commentary in significant constitutional cases from as early as 1798 to 1992. Among the cases they analyze are *Slaughterhouse, Plessy, Adair, Coppage, Gitlow, Roe, Bowers, Casey,* and *Lee.*

Editor Terry Eastland provides an illuminating introduction to the volume, and Griffin B. Bell, former attorney general of the United States, comments on the power of judicial review in a provocative forward.